THE DELA...
A FAMILY HISTORY

Revised Third Edition

MARTIN GREEN

Published by
Powdene Publicity Limited

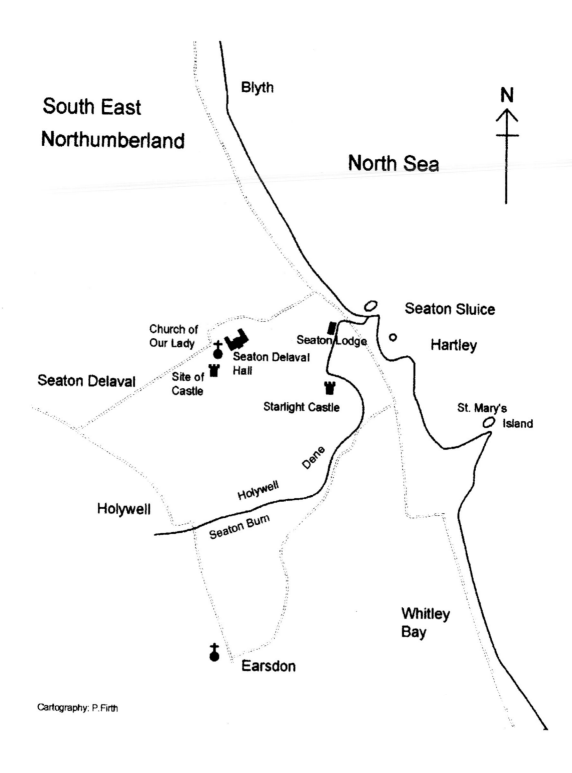

South East
Northumberland

Blyth

North Sea

N

Seaton Sluice

Hartley

Church of
Our Lady

Seaton Lodge

Seaton Delaval
Hall

Seaton Delaval

Site of
Castle

Starlight Castle

St. Mary's
Island

Dene

Holywell

Holywell

Seaton Burn

Whitley
Bay

Earsdon

Cartography: P.Firth

2

ACKNOWLEDGEMENTS

First of all I must thank Morag Horseman for reading the first draft and making helpful suggestions. I would also like to thank the staff at the Literary & Philosophical Society in Newcastle for their helpfulness in finding obscure volumes in distant parts of their wonderful library. I am also grateful to the County Records Office in Woodhorn for copying many documents from the Delaval collection. I would also like to acknowledge the help and encouragement I have received from members of Seaton Sluice Local History Society especially Peter Jubb for information on naval matters and Elspeth Gould for information on the Huthwaites.

My grateful thanks to the following for photographs and illustrations - Chris Crane, Delaval family portraits on pages 20, 66, 67, 68, 69, 72, 73, 74, 100, 102 and 104 by permission of Lord Hastings; Peter Firth, page 2 map; Ford Castle, by permission of Lady Joicey; the Doddington Hall portraits, photographed by Soo Spector, with the permission of Claire Birch; the County Records Office, Woodhorn, for documents on pages 42, 93 and 106; 1897 map, page 6, by permission of the Ordnance Survey; page 79 cartoon, National Portrait Gallery. Other photographs have been taken by i-2-i Photography and the author.

Finally, I must thank my wife, Wendy, for her endless patience during the many hours I have spent working on this book and Stewart Bonney of Powdene for helping to turn my manuscript into a book.

Martin Green
Email: mgreen2007@talktalk.net
© Martin Green

ISBN: 978-0-9926969-2-4
3rd Edition; 2014

Published by Powdene Publicity Limited
Unit 17, St. Peter's Wharf, Newcastle upon Tyne NE6 1TZ

Printed by xpresslitho, Washington, Tyne & Wear

THE DELAVALS FAMILY TREE 1700 - 1814

CAPTAIN FRANCIS BLAKE DELAVAL R.N.M.P. = RHODA, DAUGHTER OF ROBERT APREECE OF DODDINGTON
1692 - 1752   M. 1724 D. 1759

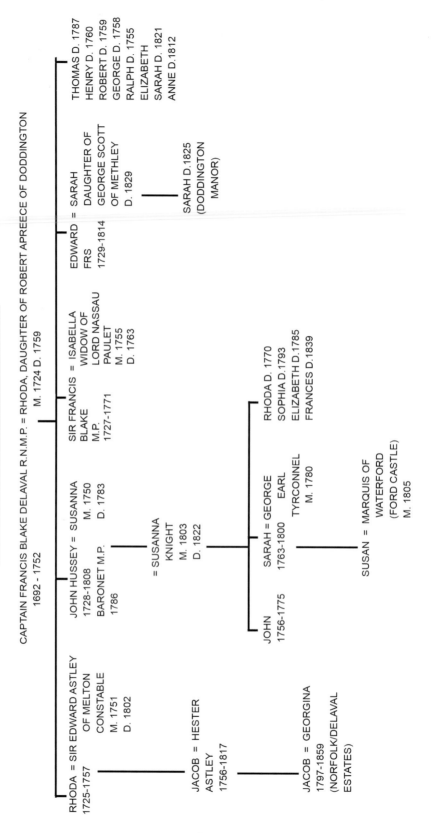

RHODA = SIR EDWARD ASTLEY
1725-1757   OF MELTON
    CONSTABLE
    M. 1751
    D. 1802

JACOB = HESTER
    ASTLEY
    1756-1817

JACOB = GEORGINA
1797-1859
(NORFOLK/DELAVAL
ESTATES)

JOHN HUSSEY = SUSANNA
1728-1808   M. 1750
BARONET M.P.   D. 1783
1786

= SUSANNA
   KNIGHT
   M. 1803
   D. 1822

JOHN
1756-1775

SARAH = GEORGE
1763-1800   EARL
    TYRCONNEL
    M. 1780

SUSAN = MARQUIS OF
    WATERFORD
    (FORD CASTLE)
    M. 1805

SIR FRANCIS = ISABELLA
BLAKE   WIDOW OF
M.P.   LORD NASSAU
1727-1771   PAULET
    M. 1755
    D. 1763

RHODA D. 1770
SOPHIA D.1793
ELIZABETH D.1785
FRANCES D.1839

EDWARD = SARAH
FRS   DAUGHTER OF
1729-1814   GEORGE SCOTT
    OF METHLEY
    D. 1829

SARAH D.1825
(DODDINGTON
MANOR)

THOMAS D. 1787
HENRY D. 1760
ROBERT D. 1759
GEORGE D. 1758
RALPH D. 1755
ELIZABETH
SARAH D. 1821
ANNE D.1812

4

CONTENTS

Martin Green is a retired primary school teacher.
He has lived in Seaton Sluice for nearly forty years.
Twelve years ago he became a guide at the Church of Our Lady,
in the grounds of Seaton Delaval Hall.

This led to an interest in all things to do with the Delavals.
Martin suffers from Parkinson's disease which unfortunately restricts his
activities but one thing he was able to do was write using a computer.
He started this book in 2006.

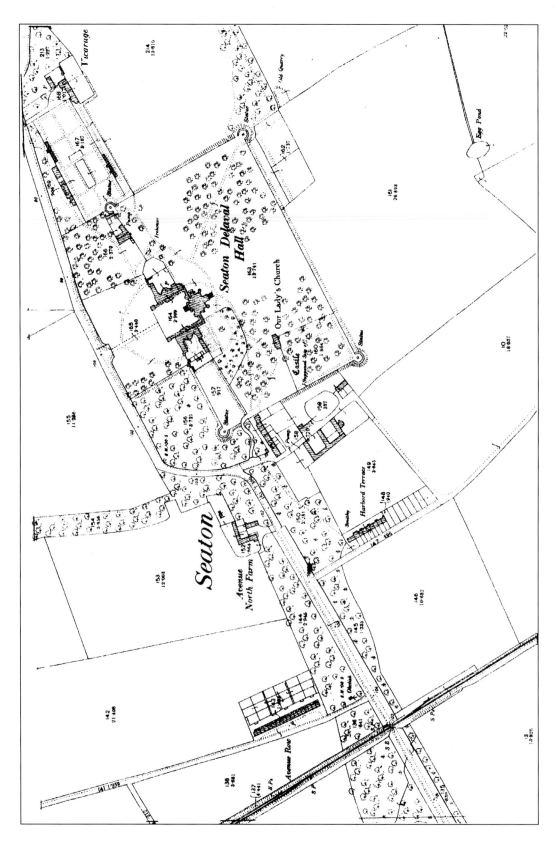

6

PREFACE

The Delavals arrived with William, Duke of Normandy, as part of his invading army in 1066. They lived at Seaton in Northumberland for the next 700 years until the last Delaval died in 1814, and they left behind a fascinating story and a unique monument in Seaton Delaval Hall. The following pages tell the story of this family, how they survived, their triumphs, their tragedies, their great achievements and their ultimate demise.

Today their legacy is evident in that superb building, Seaton Delaval Hall, now owned by the National Trust.

An early 18th century view of Delaval Hall.

Seaton Delaval Hall today.

CHAPTER ONE
FROM LAVAL TO DELAVAL

On a late summer morning in 1066 a group of knights set out from a castle at Laval in the province of Maine in France to join up with William, Duke Of Normandy, to take part in the invasion of England. Guy De Laval had married a daughter of Robert the half brother of William. It was Guy's son Hamo who took part in the invasion. William and his army killed King Harold at the Battle of Hastings in the October of 1066. William had himself crowned King of England in Westminster Abbey on Christmas Day, then began to reward those who had aided him in the conquest with land.

The South of England and the Midlands were subdued first and no doubt those closest to William were rewarded with land and estates in that part of his new kingdom. In the North of England, the native land-owning nobility continued in office for some time but as they proved to be too powerful and rebellious they were gradually replaced. In 1072 William dismissed Gospatric as Earl of Northumbria and replaced him with Waltheof, who was related to King Cnut and had married William's niece Judith. However he joined a revolt against William and was beheaded by William in 1076. The Norman Bishop of Durham was then advanced to the earldom but he was murdered in his own church by the people of Gateshead in 1080. Shortly before his death William appointed a Norman Knight, Robert de Mowbray, to the earldom. (1) In 1095 Robert quarrelled with the King, now William II, who brought an army into Northumberland and seized the Earl's castles. Bamburgh which was held by his wife resisted for some time, but she eventually yielded when the besiegers threatened to mutilate her captured husband. Robert was then taken to Windsor and imprisoned for the remaining 30 years of his life. The King then decided to abolish the earldom and, in so doing, reward the more distant members of his extended family who had helped in the conquest. So it was not until after 1095 that Northumberland finally came under Norman rule under a sheriff appointed by the King.

All land was nominally in the hands of the King and he was wise enough not to give large single blocks of land to anyone thus diminishing the chance of a recipient setting himself up as a rival. Land was given in separate parcels thus the new owner was frequently on the move visiting his scattered holdings. Because land was held in this way, it became necessary for documents to be made proving ownership, so that boundary disputes between neighbouring landowners could be settled peacefully. Courts were also set up to settle property disputes. The King did not give the land as an outright gift, in return the landowner had to pay homage to him and fight for him when required. As the new owners grew older this became very difficult, so very soon Knight's Fees were substituted. This was in effect a property tax payable to the king, and he would hire professional soldiers with the money raised.

The Delavals were granted land at Black Callerton, and Dissington in Newburn parish and at Seaton and Newsham in Earsdon parish. Documentary evidence shows that in 1212 the land at Black Callerton was worth 2 Knight's Fees, as a comparison the land held by William De Vesci at Alnwick was worth 12 Knight's Fees. In Northumberland there were 22 barons paying a total of 66 Knight's Fees. (2) The scattered nature of their landholdings was obviously inconvenient so, over time, more remote lands were sold or exchanged and estates tended to be centralised around one area.

A knight named Hubert is the first named Delaval, he is mentioned in a charter given at Winchester between 1106 and 1116 granting the tithes on his estates to the abbot of St Albans. (3) It seems odd that the tithes were paid to distant St Albans but Robert de Mowbray had quarrelled with the Bishop of Durham, William of St Calais, in 1085 and, as a result, handed Tynemouth Priory and its endowments to St Albans, thus Tynemouth Priory became a cell of St Albans. The Bishop of Durham was not happy about this and it was not until 1174 that a final settlement was reached between St. Albans and Durham concerning the status of Tynemouth Priory. At Seaton, Hubert would have found a Saxon church and a small village. He converted the stone built Saxon church into a Norman church in 1102. The north wall of the new church has a Saxon window that was saved from the old church. The now blocked up window is still clearly visible. Hubert added a choir and a sanctuary, supported by two perfect Norman arches. The church was named The Church Of Our Lady. It was officially the Delavals' private chapel but it also served as the local church for the nearby community. There was not a resident priest, so when a priest was needed one would come from Tynemouth Priory.

Hubert needed somewhere to live and he probably built a motte and bailey type of castle nearby and in the thirteenth century this had been converted into a stone tower. Initially the main branch of the family probably lived at Callerton, but very soon they made Seaton their principal home. However branches of the Delavals continued to live at Dissington and Callerton for many years. The Delavals soon started adding to their estates. By 1219 they had acquired land at Hartley from Adam of Jesmond. By the end of the century they had acquired about half the township of Holywell, adjacent to Seaton. The rest was owned by free tenants and the Scrope family. (4)

In the settlements at Seaton and Hartley, the main activity was subsistence farming and fishing. The farming system was the open field method where individuals held strips of land in two large fields, some on good land and some on the poorer land, so that the risks were spread. Fishing was the principal activity at Hartley.

We know that salt was being manufactured early in the thirteenth century at Hartley Pans, the old name for Seaton Sluice. The salt was made by boiling seawater in huge pans heated by coal. The coal was gathered, open-cast fashion, locally. When this source was exhausted, mining in bell pits was started. This name derives from the shape of the excavation. A narrow vertical shaft was sunk into the coal seam and men worked with picks and shovels to remove the coal. When the enlarged chamber started to collapse the pit would be abandoned and a new pit started nearby.

Hubert was probably succeeded by his son Robert, who was resident at Seaton. He acquired property in the manor of Eachwick, before 1138. (5) Mention of this is found in papers relating to Hexham Priory where a moiety, or half share, is granted to the Prior at Hexham. Eachwick formed part of the Dissington estate.

After Robert came Gilbert Delaval, who may have been Robert's son. (Records are not always reliable in these early years and names and dates are not necessarily correct.) Some sources claim Gilbert came from a different lineage. (6)

By the reign of King John (1199-1216) the Delavals had, like virtually all the Norman families who settled after the conquest, become English. They no longer looked back to Normandy for help and support. Their main interest was in developing their estates and they had no desire to help John fight costly wars on the continent. Many barons, including Gilbert Delaval, refused to fight for the King until their grievances had been addressed. John retaliated by seizing castles and taking hostages. It was not unusual for the King to take a son from the noble families to his court where he was held to ensure the loyalty of his parents, and one of Gilbert Delaval's sons was taken hostage. John ruled in an arbitrary and dictatorial manner and was hated because of his vindictive personality and abuse of royal patronage.

When the northern barons met at Stamfordham at Easter 1215, the Delavals were there along with the De Vescis, the De Merleys, etc. Support for the rebels grew and when London turned against the King because of his taxation policy, the end was inevitable. The barons forced John to sign The Great Charter, or Magna Carta, at Runnymede. The Delavals were there at the signing but they

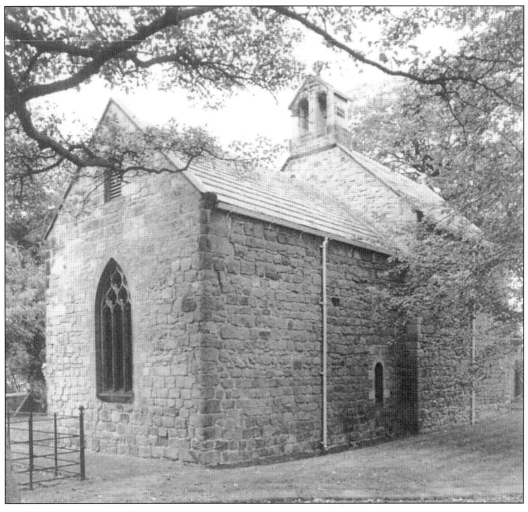

Hubert Delaval built the Church of Our Lady in 1102.

were not one of the 25 who signed on behalf of the barons. (7) The words Magna Charta (note spelling error) appear on two Delaval Hatchments to remind people of the past achievements of the Delaval family. (8)

The ink had hardly dried on the Charter before both sides were preparing for war. John had no intention of surrendering power to the barons. The northern barons allied themselves with Alexander II of Scotland who crossed the River Tweed in October 1215. This forced John to come north and on his way to Scotland he reduced the castles at Mitford and Morpeth. John then plundered the Scottish lowlands to punish Alexander for supporting the northern barons many of whom fled or submitted. (9) What Gilbert Delaval did is not known but in October of 1216 John died. By 1219 Gilbert had made his peace with the new King, Henry III, and was asked to serve on a Royal Commission. Gilbert died about 1229 having held the barony for 63 years.

Notes on chapter one.

1. *County History, Vol IX, p136. Also Eyewitness, by E. Miller, p26. The siege of Bamburgh Castle 1095 from Anglo-Saxon Chronicle.*

2. *Archaeologia Aeliana (A.A.) Vol XXX, p16*

3. *A tithe was a tenth of one's income and everyone was required to pay this to the church. Northumberland Families, p145*

4. *North-East England in the Middle Ages, by R. Lomas, p184*

5. *County of Conflict Northumberland, by R. Lomas, p74*

6. *Northumberland Families,Vol. 1 Percy Hedley. This book contains a much more comprehensive account of the family in the 12th to 16th centuries together with extensive family trees, p145 - p154.*

7. *A.A. Vol. 12, p216*

8. *A Hatchment shows the armorial bearings of a deceased person. There are six hatchments in The Church of Our Lady at Seaton.*

9. *About twenty Northumbrian Barons rebelled against King John. Their leader was Eustace de Vesci of Alnwick. Only two Northumbrian barons supported the king. County of Conflict Northumberland, p166.*

CHAPTER TWO
PROSPERITY THEN BANKRUPTCY

The Delavals continued to prosper and to play a part in administering the area. Sir Henry Delaval held the barony in 1258 when the property at Black Callerton, North Dissington, Seaton, Hartley and Holywell was worth £142 19s. 8d. Sir Henry served as a Border Commissioner and a Justice of the Assize in 1250. However as the century progressed raids by Scottish Reivers reduced the value of the property. In the 14th century the country was ravaged by the Black Death. Many people died, whole communities were wiped out and the value of Delaval property fell to £59 17s. 6d. Ten cottages in Hartley were in ruins and fields were left uncultivated because there was nobody to work them. (1)

Twice during the next century the Delaval line nearly died out. Sir Robert Delaval had three sons but none of them had children who lived to be adults, so it appeared that when his last son, William, died in 1388, the estates would pass to Sir Robert's sister, Alice, wife of John de Whitchester. Thus it seemed that the Delaval Estates would pass into the hands of the Whitchesters, but their children also died so eventually William's cousin, John Delaval of Newsham, inherited the estates.

In 1423 John made a settlement of his lands on his daughter Elizabeth who had married a lawyer, John Woodman, alias Horsley, (he adopted the name Horsley because he owned land at Horsley.) Elizabeth died before 1456 and her son 'James De La Val of Seaton de la Val otherwise called James Horsley' inherited the Newsham property and eventually the Seaton estates. In 1469, James's succession was disputed by the Sheriff of Northumberland, Marquis Montague, and for a time James was imprisoned and forced to release his rights. When Montague was killed in the battle of Barnet on Easter Day 1471, James's rights were restored. James Horsley used the name Delaval, rather than his father's name of Horsley, and his four sons also adopted the name Delaval, so the Delaval name survived. The practice of using the mother's name was not uncommon. (2)

The centre of the Delaval Estate was now firmly fixed on Seaton with its manor house and about 600 acres of estate land plus a tenant population of twenty-six bondsmen and thirty cottages. In neighbouring Hartley, the Delavals had about 100 acres of arable land plus four bondsmen with 24 acres each and fifteen cottages. Newsham probably had a similar structure. In Dissington there was a manor house with about 300 acres of estate arable land and 32 acres of meadow land as well as ten bondsmen each with 24 acres of land and twenty cottages. No records have survived for Black Callerton but its structure would have been similar to Dissington. (3) The families at Dissington and Seaton remained on close terms and, as we shall see later, the Dissington branch saved the family name from extinction.

During the reign of Henry VIII the country was convulsed by the reformation. Henry broke away from the Roman Catholic Church and established the English Protestant Church with himself as head. It soon became clear that anyone supporting Catholicism faced persecution or death. The Delavals, in the person of Sir John Delaval, took the prudent step and changed the way they practised their religion. The Church of Our Lady became a Protestant church but no one bothered to change the name, so today it is a Protestant church with a "Catholic" name. Sir John who died in 1562, took a prominent part in administering the area. He was five times Sheriff of the county the last being in 1554. (The Sheriff was the Crown's chief agent in the county.) Sir John's grandson, Sir Robert, also served for a time as Sheriff and Border Commissioner. In 1571 he married Dorothy, the daughter of Ralph Gray of Chillingham. A piece of the wedding regalia celebrating the marriage between the Grays and the Delavals is displayed in the Church of Our Lady.

In March 1603 Queen Elizabeth I died and James VI of Scotland became James I of England. In theory the lawless border area should have ceased to be a problem, but of course trouble did not end overnight. It took several years before raiding and thieving ceased and peace came to Northumberland. This brought changes to the rural economy. Farmers knew that they could plant crops and harvest them without harassment, wasteland was brought back into production and farm rents could go up. At Hartley around 1610 Sir Ralph Delaval, great grandson of Sir John, completed the task begun by his father of converting the 2,500-acre estate at Hartley from arable to pasture for sheep. Unfortunately the sheep succumbed to disease so he began the practice of renting out the estate land to tenants. Thus the estate became a mixture of managed estate land and tenanted farms similar to the layout today. (4)

Sir Ralph lived in the old tower and attached a Tudor manor house at Seaton. He refurbished the house, added new windows and built a new brew house. With an income of over £1,000 per year the Delavals were considered one of the seven principal families in the county. (5) As one of the leading Protestant gentlemen Sir Ralph enjoyed Royal patronage and served on a commission to deal with recusants, i.e., people – mainly Roman Catholics – who refused to go to Protestant church services.

Sir Ralph's lifestyle was recorded by his son: 'he kept an open great and plentiful house for entertainment of his own family consisting daily of three score persons and above…. His life was religious. He kept a chaplain ever in his house that read public prayers daily and preached each Sunday in his chapel and taught and educated his children. He governed his people in excellent order and stocked and managed his whole estate himself, directing his servants daily their several labours…. He never rid to any public assembly without five or six men in liveries and two or three of his sons to attend him. He never affected drinking. Cards or dice he could never abide them. His apparel ever decent not rich. He was a man of voluble tongue, excellent discourse and of good memory. He understood the Latin and Greek tongues…He loved hunting, but left it off long ere he died.' (6) He expired in 1628 and was buried in his chapel, the Church of Our Lady.

When he died his estate brought in about £1,991 per year but expenditure in mortgage, annuities, wages and rents was about £1,000. The surplus was not enough to satisfy his widow and sons. Things came to a head when his widow married the estates manager, Francis Reed, and the sons threatened to kill him if he remained at Seaton. Lady Delaval and her new husband removed their possessions to Horton and her action reduced the estate to comparative penury. It was her grandson, also called Ralph, who restored the estate to prosperity.

In 1644 during the English Civil War, Newcastle was besieged by a Scottish army under the command of General Alexander Leslie, Earl of Leven. The Scots had formed an alliance with the Parliamentarians against the Royalists led by King Charles I. Leven's army was strong and well organised. This war, like most conflicts in the 17th century, was about power. Who ruled - King or Parliament - and of course religion.

The Scots wanted to reform the Anglican Church on Presbyterian lines. Royalists regarded the Scottish intervention as an attack on the very fabric of Anglicanism. The Scots saw an opportunity to interfere and promote their cause. In January 1644 they crossed the Tweed on the 19th and by the end of the month they were outside the walls of Newcastle. However the gates were firmly shut against them. The Mayor of Newcastle, Sir John Marley, made it perfectly clear that they were not going to abandon their allegiance to the King or surrender the city. Disappointed, Leven left a small force to blockade the city and marched south to subdue Royalist opposition in Durham and York. The blcokade stopped all shipping on the Tyne including the exporting of coal to London. By August Royalist opposition in the north had virtually ceased. Only Newcastle held out. It was protected by its medieval walls and defended by about 1500 men. Not all were regular soldiers. Leven had about 7,000 assault troops. The defenders were offered generous terms if they would surrender but the Mayor rejected all attempts at compromise. Pressure was mounting on

Leven and in London they were desperate to get Tyne coal before winter set in. So on October 19th, after heavy artillery bombardment, the Scottish infantry assaulted the walls and took the city. There was considerable destruction and loss of life. The Scottish soldiers were, however, well disciplined and soon restored order. There was huge relief in London when the coal trade resumed. Parliament put the civil administration of Newcastle in local hands while the Scots were in control of military matters. It was not until 1647 that the Scots finally withdrew and left Newcastle. Just ten days before Newcastle fell Parliament appointed several new Deputy County Lieutenants for Northumberland. One of them was Ralph Delaval. He got on so well with the Scottish invaders that he married Leven's daughter, Ann, the widow of Hugh Fraser, in St. Nicholas Cathedral on April 2nd, 1646. (7)

The Civil War dragged on until 1649 when Parliament tried and executed King Charles I. This was a step too far for many people including Ralph Delaval. The Scots were also against the execution of the King and they fell out with Cromwell over this. Oliver Cromwell, by now virtually a dictator, wouldn't tolerate dissent. He turned on his former allies and led his army into Scotland and massacred 3,000 Scots at Dunbar. Leven, travelling with a very small escort, unfortunately ran into a platoon of English dragoons and was taken prisoner. He was put in the Tower of London where it was the custom for relatives to provide the 'necessaries' for wealthy prisoners. As Ralph Delaval was his son-in-law he provided them. In October 1651 Ralph got permission to take Leven to Delaval Hall where he was to be confined and treated as a prisoner of war. He had to lodge securities of £20,000 and he was not allowed to travel more than 12 miles from Delaval Hall. So the conqueror of Newcastle returned to the North East as a prisoner where he was looked after by his daughter. Fortunately for Leven his confinement did not last long and he was returned to London in 1652. Meanwhile Ralph continued to prosper. In 1659 he entered Richard Cromwell's Parliament as member for Northumberland. Royalists described him as a 'marvellous honest gentleman.' After the restoration of the monarchy in 1660, Charles II made Ralph a baronet. (8)

As well as managing the farming estate, Ralph also took a keen interest in the collieries and salt pans. The demand for coal increased as cities like London expanded and the first stirrings of the industrial revolution occurred.

The harbour at Seaton was unable to handle the shipping needed to meet this demand because its north facing entrance was difficult to navigate, so Ralph set about improving the harbour. He built a pier to protect the entrance, but this was soon swept away, so he built a second pier and cemented the stone blocks together to strengthen it, but this too was soon swept away. After a lot of thought he tried again. The third time he joined every block of stone to the next with a dovetail joint so that when the tide surged against the pier the blocks lifted then fell back into place. This pier erected around 1670 protected the harbour entrance for many years, allowing ships to enter and leave the port more easily. (9) However the harbour was still too shallow to allow fully loaded ships to leave port; often ships loaded the last of their cargo out at sea, manhandling the coal out of smaller vessels. To overcome this problem of the harbour silting up an ingenious system for cleaning the silt out was devised. Huge gates were built across Seaton burn and at high tide these were closed damming the flow of water from upstream.

As the tide went out the muddy bottom of the harbour was exposed and this was then ploughed up by horse drawn ploughs. When the mud was broken up the gates were opened and the harbour was sluiced out by the pent up water, so deepening the harbour. Thus the port of Seaton became Seaton Sluice. This ingenious system was admired by many visitors to the area including the great eighteenth century engineer John Smeaton. (10) As a result of these improvements, which cost Sir Ralph over £7,000, Charles II granted Sir Ralph the right to be collector and surveyor of his own port, thus freeing him from interference from Newcastle or Blyth. Encouraged by this recognition Sir Ralph appears to have built a pier on the west side of the entrance having been offered a grant of £1,500 towards it by the King. Unfortunately the King died shortly afterwards and only £500 was ever paid. In 1685 fourteen vessels used the harbour and 56 cargoes of coal and salt were shipped out. (11)

Ships were also in danger from French and Dutch privateers, so to protect the harbour from attack Sir Ralph installed a gun battery. It was used at least once, when, in 1667, shots were fired to scare off a Dutch privateer.

Sir Ralph's eldest son, Robert, married Lady Elizabeth Livingston, daughter of Viscount Newburgh in the Scottish peerage, in July 1670. Elizabeth was about twenty-one when she married. She had been brought up by her aunt, Lady Stanhope, as her parents had to flee abroad for supporting the Royalists in the civil war. When she was about fourteen, after the restoration of the monarchy, she was found a position at court as a maid of the privy chamber. Lady Elizabeth was pretty and well connected and her aunt wanted her to marry. She was courted by several suitors but Elizabeth rejected them all. One because he was not rich enough, a second because he was a catholic and another probably simply to spite her aunt. At this point Sir Ralph Delaval suggested his son Robert should marry Elizabeth, and she accepted his proposal. From the start they had a difficult relationship, she never developed passionate or even friendly feelings for her husband while Robert aspired to be a restoration rake and a drunkard. Elizabeth tried to change his habits but failed. So this unhappy and childless marriage continued until Robert died in 1682. Elizabeth had never liked Seaton and after her husband died there was nothing to keep her there so she moved back to Lincolnshire. (12)

Soon after Robert died, Sir Ralph's second son also died. In 1684 his third son, also called Ralph, married Diana Booth, daughter of George Lord Delamere. The family were well off at this time and so to ensure that any daughter of the union could make a good marriage a clause was put into the marriage contract granting a dowry of £8,000 to a daughter on her marriage.

The elder Sir Ralph moved out of the old Delaval mansion in 1685 and into Seaton Lodge, a thatched house overlooking Seaton burn. Sir Ralph died there in 1691 and his son Ralph died five years later leaving Diana a widow with a young daughter. So by 1699 the estate was in decline. Ralph's personal estate went to pay creditors, while the property at Seaton Delaval and Hartley passed to his widow Diana.

The rest of the estate went to Sir John Delaval, another son of Sir Ralph. John lived at Seaton Lodge. (13) Hoping to improve her situation Diana married Sir Edward Blackett and two months later her only daughter, also called Diana, aged just thirteen, married Edward's son, William Blackett. This was not a love match! Sir Edward claimed the £8,000 marriage dowry, as in the 1684 marriage settlement, but the 1684 document had been badly drawn and the money to pay the dowry was tied up in the estate until the bride's parents died. So the dowry was not paid.

In 1713 the elder Diana died and Sir John Delaval tried to reclaim the Delaval estates. The Blacketts' resisted and demanded the marriage settlement be paid, which with interest had now risen to over £14,624. Sir John could not pay it without selling off a large part of the estate and his son-in-law, John Rogers of Denton, strongly opposed this.

Sir Edward then petitioned the court of Chancery for an order to sell Seaton Delaval and Hartley manor. In effect, he would seize the Delaval estates and bankrupt Sir John (14).

Notes on chapter two.

1. *County History Vol. IX, p146*

2. *Northumberland Families, p148*

3. *N.E. England in the Middle Ages, by R. Lomas, p184*

4. *From Border to Middle Shire: Northumberland, 1586-1625, p170*

5. *IBID p63*

6. *County History,Vol. 1X, p158*

7. *A.A. Vol. 12 p222, The Great Siege of Newcastle by R Serdiville and J Sadler.*

8. *Men of Mark, Vol. II, p38. The Surtees Society 1978, p11*

9. *Ports and Harbours of Northumberland, by Stafford Linsley, p175*

10. *John Smeaton drew up plans in 1758 for enlarging the harbour at Seaton Sluice. He proposed building a north facing wall out from the beach but this was never built, Delaval Papers, p159*

11. *Ports and Harbours, p175*

12. *The Meditations of Lady Elizabeth Delaval, edited by D.G.Greene Published by the Surtees Society 1978, p9-17. Lady Elizabeth wrote a series of meditations during her teenage years and these deeply religious tracts are published in the above volume.*

13. *In 1696 Sir John Delaval claimed that Seaton Lodge was the finest thatched house in the kingdom. The Old Halls and Houses of Northumberland p230.*

14. *Northumberland Families, p153 County History, VOL. IX, p162*

CHAPTER THREE
SAVING THE DELAVAL ESTATES

Admiral Sir Ralph Delaval, knighted in 1690, by Sir Godfrey Kneller.

It was Admiral George Delaval from the Dissington branch of the family who saved the Delaval estates.

The younger son of George Delaval of Dissington, he entered the Royal Navy under the patronage of a distant cousin, Sir Ralph Delaval, who had joined the navy around 1672. In May 1690 Sir Ralph was deputed by the officers of the fleet to present a loyal address to William and Mary and for this he was knighted and promoted to Vice Admiral, and in June of that year he commanded the rear squadron at the battle of Beachy Head. In 1692 his flag was on the Royal Sovereign, a magnificent 100 gun ship, and he fought at the battle of La Hogue when 16 French ships were destroyed. In 1694 Sir Ralph, along with admirals Killingrew and Shovell, was in charge of the fleet when, because of poor intelligence and bad luck, the French were able to capture a convoy of merchant ships in the Bay of Biscay. Public opinion was enraged and Delaval and Killingrew were accused of being in league with the French. This was shown to be untrue and eventually his name was cleared, but Delaval never went to sea again. In 1695 he retired from the navy and was elected as a Tory MP for Great Bedwin in Wiltshire. He left Parliament at the next election in 1698 and lived quietly in retirement until his death in January 1707. He was buried in Westminster Abbey, with the reputation 'of a great and gallant officer and a generous and hospitable man'. (1)

Meanwhile George was furthering his career. In 1695 he was promoted Captain of HMS Oxford, a 54-gun fourth rate ship. He sailed to the Mediterranean where he combined his naval career with a diplomatic mission as an envoy to the Emperor of Fez and Morocco. He was ordered to go to Tangiers to negotiate the release of British ships seized by the Emperor and seek compensation for the loss of cargoes and equipment. He concluded a treaty in 1700 for the redemption of British captives and in 1708 an agreement was reached not to molest each other's ships. In 1710 he was advanced to became envoy to the King of Portugal and was away for more than three years. On his return, he became an MP. He was elected in 1715 as member for West Looe and records show that he always voted with the government. (2) He continued with his naval career and in 1718 he was appointed a Rear Admiral. His diplomatic and naval work had enabled him to amass a considerable fortune.

Just when George became aware of the difficulties Sir John was having at Seaton with Sir Edward Blackett is not clear, but he soon made up his mind that the Delaval estate would not be sold to the Blacketts. Negotiations to buy the estate started in 1716. In January 1717 George writes to his brother: 'I am answering your letter of the 15inst. We are still talking of Seaton; but Sir Edward does not descend and I do not mount. I fancy a mediator might bring us together but ye Knight has no friends. My neighbour Aisleby lives within six miles of him and they never see each other.' But in March 1717 George was able again to write to his brother and said: 'You'll judge what is necessary to be done immediately at Seaton. I suppose making the house water tight. Sir Edward promises to write to his Steward this Post to give you possession for me'. (3) So George had acquired the old Seaton mansion and paid off the Blacketts. Sir John retired to live in Seaton Lodge, but he retained a life interest in the Seaton and Hartley estate until his death in 1729.

George did not immediately retire from the sea. As he said in a letter to his brother: 'I consider my estate will not bring much superfluous money, and I would be glad to divert my self a little in my old age in repairing the old house making a garden and planting forest trees. I must go to sea that I may be secured. If I become Admiral I shall have £156 per annum half pay and go to my retreat with honour and advantage.' (4) Part of 1718 was spent at sea aboard the Royal Oak, however he was already thinking of what he wanted to do with his new estate. In a letter to his brother he writes: 'I intend to persuade Sir John Vanbrugh to see Seaton if possible, and to give me a plan of a house or to alter the old one, which he is most excellent at; and if he cannot come, he'll recommend a man at York who understands these matters'. (5)

Vanbrugh was one of the leading architects of his time but he did not come into the profession until he was in his thirties. Born in 1664 in London of Flemish descent, he was commissioned in the army in 1686 and spent some time in France, including a period in the Bastille where he was held on suspicion of spying. He continued his military career on his return to England in 1692, where he was commissioned into the marines but by 1696 he had become a dramatist. He wrote two argumentative and outspoken Restoration comedies, The Relapse and in 1697, The Provoked Wife. These plays offended many sections of society, not only by their sexual explicitness but also by their message in defence of women's rights in marriage. So disturbed by the reaction to his plays and the problems in producing them, in 1698, after meeting Nicholas Hawksmoor, he turned his energies to architecture. He had no formal training but it has been suggested that he did study architecture while he was in France. In 1699, with the help of Hawksmoor, he started to design Castle Howard for Lord Carlisle. (6) In 1702 with the help of Lord Carlisle he got the job of comptroller of the King's Works making him second only to Sir Christopher Wren in the field of official architecture.

Vanbrugh's most important commission came in 1705 when he was asked to design and build Blenheim Palace, the nation's gift to the Duke of Marlbrough. He built a superb Palace but it caused him endless trouble and he never saw it finished. Admiral George who had seen Castle Howard and liked it, approached Vanbrugh about repairing the old building at Seaton. Vanbrugh came to Seaton and decided it was beyond repair. He suggested that the site be cleared, and offered to design and build a splendid new house for Admiral George, an offer he couldn't refuse. Vanbrugh drew up the plans for Seaton Delaval Hall, (these have unfortunately been lost) and work started in 1718.

Notes on chapter three.

1. *Men Of Mark Twixt Tyne And Tees, Welford, 1895, Vol 2, p48*

2. *The House of Commons 1715-1754, by R. Sedgwick, p609*

3. *Delaval Papers, by J. Robinson, p119-120*

4. *Delaval Papers p11*

5. *Delaval Papers p121*

6. *Nicholas Hawksmoor was one of the most original English Baroque architects.*
    He worked with Vanbrugh on Castle Howard and Blenheim Palace.

CHAPTER FOUR
BUILDING DELAVAL HALL

The Great Hall and Gallery.

Vanbrugh designed Delaval Hall but he rarely visited the site and it was built by local workers under the supervision of a Mr Mewburne. There are also references to a Mr Etty, who was probably William Etty, an architect or master mason from York. He is probably the man referred to in the letter quoted in Chapter 3. Work started on the hall in 1718, the old medieval buildings were cleared and the only building left standing was the Church of Our Lady.

A bill dated October 1720 stated: 'to cash paid - the several charges and expenses of mason work, and labourers pulling down Seaton Old House as well as building a new mansion house from 2nd April 1720 to 2nd October 1720 - £426 14s 10d.' (1) The stone to build the hall was quarried locally, a letter from Mewburne in September 1719 says: 'The work at the quarry goes currently on with only four workmen and about eight labourers. The way from the quarry to the House was never so good this summer'. (2)

Documents show that around 1720, some 220 men were employed building the hall and laying out the estate. In the quarry there were 30 quarrymen, paid 1s 6d per day, also 13 labourers paid 8d per day, and 22 men were employed leading stone from the quarry at 6d per load.

Wages were the main expenditure as virtually everything was made or supplied on site. The stone came from local quarries and most of the timber from estate woodlands. The mortar to bind the stone together, was made by mixing lime with sand and water. The lime was obtained by burning local limestone in lime kilns the remains of which are still visible in Seaton Sluice. Nails were made by a local blacksmith. Only glass for the 300 plus windows would have been brought in. (3)

Employed in building the hall were 38 masons and joiners at 1s 6d and 1s 4d per day, also 32 labourers at 8d per day. In the plantations 18 men were employed planting and tying trees and renewing quicks (hedge plants) at 8d per day, while 12 women were paid 4d per day for weeding and watering the same. Records show that 400 lime trees were planted, 200 oaks, 180 English elms and 80 Dutch elms.

Vanbrugh had not just designed a house but a whole new landscape much of which is still in evidence today. Building the hall provided employment for people over a wide area. 4d a day was paid to: 'The bell woman at Shields to give notice to labourers who maybe employed at Seaton Delaval in Hedging and Trenching ground'. (4) Presumably the bell woman's job was to wake up the labourers in the early morning. Work progressed and in 1721 Vanbrugh wrote: 'The admiral is very gallant in his operation not being disposed to starve the design at all so he is like to have a very fine dwelling for himself now and fore his nephew here after'. (5)

The design Vanbrugh drew up was similar to that employed at Castle Howard and Blenheim; a centre block between two arcaded and pedimented wings. However Seaton Delaval is on a much smaller scale. The principal block contains, as at Castle Howard and Blenheim, the main state and living rooms, and forms the centre of a three-sided court, 180 feet deep and 150 feet wide. Towers crowned by balustrades and pinnacles give the house something of what Vanbrugh called his 'castle air'. The centre block is about 75 feet square with octagonal towers added to the four corners. On each side is a stair tower lit by Venetian windows linking the corridor which runs around the rear of the house to the wings. The east wing contains the stables, the west wing houses the kitchens. Rustic stonework is used across the entire façade; around the main doorway at the top of a flight of steps the twin columns are stark and yet ornamental, as they provide no structural use. The whole house has a severe and sombre atmosphere yet it fits perfectly into the Northumbrian landscape. Vanbrugh is said to have been inspired by one of Palladio's Italian masterpieces. The style is referred to as English Baroque yet it is uniquely Vanbrugh.

Looking at the wings, the arched links add to the perspective of the courtyard, the upper windows are square-headed but the centre three bays project forward, have round-headed windows and are crowned with a pediment. The wings are terminated with a square block with long round-headed windows and crowned with urns. Turning to the south or garden front this is more restrained than the north; the entrance is up a flight of steps through an elegant portico between four Ionic columns topped with a pedimented frieze and balustrade. Standing on these steps one sees the genius of Vanbrugh's landscape design; in the middle distance is a perfectly situated obelisk, the rest is a tranquil rural scene of trees and fields all carefully set out to hide the surrounding settlements. The whole site is protected by a ha-ha wall raised at the corners into circular bastions, which at one time contained statues. (6) The lord is the master of all he sees!

One can only admire Vanbrugh's work from the outside as the interior was destroyed by fire in 1822. The best description of what the interior was like when it was built, is given by Mackenzie writing in 1825: 'The first room which you enter is a most stately hall 44ft long 44ft high. Numerous arches, recesses and niches, please the informed observer, more with the harmony of their proportions than with the splendour of their decorations. The floor is of black and white marble, and the chimney piece finely adapted to the style of the room; the figures which support it are exquisitely executed. Opposite to the door is a grand music gallery, faced with elegant iron balustrades upon a fine entablature and supported by beautiful consoles: in the uppermost niches are statues as large as life, admirably executed by the best Italian artists, with their attitudes and symbols representing Music, Painting, Geography, Sculpture, Architecture and Astronomy. The ceiling is extremely elegant, to the right and left passages paved with marble lead through lofty arches to handsome rooms wainscoted with mahogany in which are the pictures of Admiral Delaval and others of Lord Delaval's ancestors…and also to the two grand winding geometrical stone staircases 17ft in diameter reaching from the bottom to the top of the house…having iron balustrades of a very light and elegant form.

The hall leads to a splendid saloon, fronting the pleasure-grounds, 75ft long, and from the door at which you enter to the folding glass door on the opposite side, it is 30ft wide. In this room are eight majestic fluted Corinthian columns of the most beautiful stone, and the same number of pilasters which divide it up in to three spaces; the ceiling was executed by the famous Italian artist Vercelli, and is exquisitely modelled, and admirably coloured. At the east end is a small antechamber which leads into a spacious drawing room and also into a lesser drawing room contiguous to an elegant eating room, beautifully ornamented with festoons of fruit and flowers…so admirably painted as perfectly to resemble nature. Most of the best rooms have marble chimney pieces of admirable workmanship.' (7)

As in all Vanbrugh's houses the principal floor is supported by a vaulted basement of almost Cyclopean strength. Today the basement is dark, eerie and deserted but in the time of the Delavals this area was used for storage, wine cellars, pantries, a strong room, coal storage and so on.

Until the death of Sir Edward Astley, 22nd Lord Hastings, in 2007, the west wing contained his private apartments and, on the upper floor, a picture gallery containing paintings of members of the Delaval family, together with some of the original furniture.

The east wing contains the cathedral-like stables. The grandeur of these vast stalls, with monolithic mangers and ashlar stone partitions, are one of the most impressive things here. They were built by Sir Francis Blake Delaval, after being inspired by visiting Lord Hopetoun's estate in Scotland in 1765, where there are similar grand stables.

We can follow the building of the hall by looking at the old account books. We can see that the kitchens were nearly finished by October 1723 because £2 5s is paid to Joseph Green for setting up a clock in the kitchen. Money paid to Mr Etty showed he visited the site for 17 days in April 1723, for 10 days in June 1724, and for 3 days in August 1724 with Sir John Vanbrugh. (8) In a bundle of accounts at the Records Office, is a document which says: ' The whole cost of building Delaval Hall from the beginning to 3rd April 1725 - £6,262 11s 3d. (9) Thus, after seven years, expenditure was less than £1,000 per year. After ten years the cost for the basic building would be around £10,000, then, if adding in the cost of painted ceilings, ornate plaster work, mahogany panelling (10) and marble floors, £12,000 would seem a reasonable outlay for building Delaval Hall. (11)

By 1730 the Hall was built very much as it is seen today but looking at some 18th century pictures of Delaval Hall one is struck by the number of pictures showing structures which are no longer there. An oil painting by Arthur Pond in 1745 clearly shows a second storey connecting the main block to the kitchen or west wing. This structure has completely disappeared. The matching structure on the east wing was destroyed in the 1822 fire. The late Lord Hastings explained that this painting and others like it were just an architect's design showing how the Hall could be improved. It was difficult to argue against this because there is no evidence on site of any building work. Recently some local historians have questioned this explanation and suggested that these buildings were built and within a few years were demolished. It is difficult to reason why these buildings were removed within a short time, but careful examination of the existing structure has provided evidence that some stonework - where the missing wing would have joined up to the main building - has been expertly replaced. Documental evidence is sparse and inconclusive. The arguement may not be solved until convincing archaeological evidence is found by excavation.

In June 1723 Admiral George Delaval fell from his horse and died a few days later, leaving his estate and the unfinished hall to his nephew, Captain Francis Blake Delaval. With Vanbrugh's death in 1726, it meant that neither of the men who had helped create the hall would see their work finished. The hall is a suitable memorial to the far-sighted Admiral who commissioned it and it has been described as Vanbrugh's masterpiece. A building that 'appeals to the emotions as well as the intellect'. The last word goes to Vanbrugh: 'One may find a great deal of pleasure in building a palace for an other when one should find very little in living in it oneself'. (12)

Definition of some Architectural terms used.

Ashlar *a fashioned block of stone built into a wall.*

Arcaded *a series of arches free standing or built into a wall.*

Balustrade *a short post in a series supporting a rail.*

Column *an upright pillar circular in plan usually tapering, designed to carry a load.*

Doric, Ionic, Corinthian *style of column based on classical Greek architecture which get progressively slimmer and more ornate.*

Frieze *a horizontal band of ornamental stonework.*

Ha-ha *a trench or ditch often lined with stone which forms a boundary to a site. As it is below ground it does not interrupt the view.*

Palladian *after the style of the Italian architect Palladio, whose dignified and graceful buildings were much regarded in the 18th century.*

Pediment *a triangular area over a portico or above a window.*

Pilaster *a column attached to a wall and projecting from it.*

Portico *a large formal entrance porch with a roof supported with columns.*

Rustic *stonework with a rough texture often cut with deep grooves.*

Venetian Window *a window in three sections with the central part higher than the others.*

Wainscot *the timber lining to walls.*

Notes on chapter four.

1. *Delaval Papers, p9*

2. *ibid, p122*

3. *Local tradition says there is a window for each day of the year. The Window Tax for 1788 paid for 300 windows. Tax paid was £38 11s. Delaval Papers, p135*

4. *ibid, p124*

5. *ibid, p13*

6. *Pevsner, p563. Ridgeway in his book suggests that the Ha-ha and bastions had a military significance and could be used as an artillery platform to defend the house! Sir John Vanbrugh and Landscape Architecture, p60. The statues have been moved into the gardens.*

7. *An Historic Topographical and Descriptive View of Northumberland by Mackenzie, 1825, p418*

8. *Delaval Papers, p124*

9. *C.R.O. 2/DE/13/11*

10 *From letters that Mewburne wrote, we know that the Mahogany Room was built in 1726. Using mahogany for panelling was unusual in the early years of the 18th century. Vanbrugh – His Work in the North, D. Anderson, p82*

11. *The only other major expenditure was the extension added to the south east corner of the Centre Block around 1770 at a cost of £3,175. This extension was destroyed in the 1822 fire. C.R.O. 2DE/4/4/56(b)*

12. *Sir John Vanbrugh, Storyteller in Stone by Vaughan Hart 2008, p10*

CHAPTER FIVE
FROM FORD TO DODDINGTON

With the death of Admiral George Delaval we will leave Seaton and move to Ford Castle near the Anglo-Scottish border.

In 1338 Ford Castle had been fortified by Sir William Heron, High Sheriff of Northumberland. It was here that James IV is said to have spent some time before the Battle of Flodden, infatuated by the charms of Lady Heron while her husband, also called William, was absent. In September 1513 James led his army out of Ford to be massacred at Flodden Field.

After the battle the castle was set on fire and left in a ruinous state. When Leland visited the castle between 1535 and 1543 he described the castle as 'metly strong but in decay.' (1) William Heron's daughter married Thomas Carr and ownership passed from the Herons to the Carr family in 1536.

In 1660 the young Thomas Carr was murdered by his stepfather, John Ratcliffe of Alnwick. The Ford estate then passed to his three sisters, one of whom, Elizabeth, married Sir Francis Blake in 1662. By 1685 Sir Francis had bought out the other two sisters and owned the whole estate. Francis became M.P. for Berwick in 1688 and in 1700 he was made a Knight. Elizabeth and Francis had two daughters, one of whom was called Mary. Mary's first husband, Ralph Orde, died and she then married Edward Delaval of Dissington, the brother of Admiral George. They had a son whom they named Francis Delaval.

The admiral never married so his nephew Francis was named as his heir. Sir Francis Blake left his wife a life interest in the Ford estate, and on her death his grandson Francis would inherit the estate. Mary died in 1711, so on the death of his grandfather in 1717, Francis Delaval inherited the Ford Estate on the condition that he changed his name to Blake. So Francis Delaval became Francis Blake, but when Admiral George died and he inherited Seaton Delaval, he became Francis Blake Delaval! (2)

The other members of the Blake family were not happy with this arrangement. They would have preferred Mary's sister to inherit Ford because they knew Francis would much rather live in the newly built Delaval Hall than the dilapidated Ford Castle. Thus the legend of the curse of the Delavals came into being. It was said that the ram's head, part of the family crest, set above the main entrance to the castle, declared: 'no male Delaval would die in bed while they held both Ford and Seaton estates.' (3) And of course this is what happened! It was not until after 1806 when Sir John Delaval split the estate up in his will, that the Delavals were able to die in peace again.

Prior to gaining his inheritance, Francis, like his uncle, joined the navy and by 1714 he was a lieutenant aboard His Majesty's Ship The Lyon. Then he abruptly resigned his commission and came ashore. (4)

It seems that the family, and the government, wanted a candidate to fight for the Northumberland seat in Parliament vacated by Tom Foster. Foster had been expelled from the House of Commons for taking part in the 1715 Jacobite rebellion. One Oley Douglas put himself forward as a candidate and lobbied the Whig administration to get their backing. When John Delaval heard this he wrote to Admiral George: 'I shall consult with you what proper methods to take in order to have one of the family to oppose so scandalous a pretender as Douglas'. Meanwhile Douglas was expressing his satisfaction at the 'Good news received from Lancashire', i.e. the defeat of the Jacobites at Preston and declaring his intention to prevent the Tories: 'setting up a new member in this county'. (5)

However it seems that the Whig ministers disliked Douglas just as much as the Delavals. Both Sir John Delaval and Francis were considered as candidates but with the backing of Lord Carlisle, a minister in the Whig administration and owner of Castle Howard, it was decided Francis would be the better candidate because of his links to Ford Castle and the north of the county.

At the election the following February Francis received 832 votes. His opponent, Oley Douglas, had 809 votes. Douglas disputed the result claiming that Francis was not qualified to stand, but counsel for Francis argued he was qualified as he was the heir to his father's estate with rental income of £664 per year. The House of Commons agreed and Francis was declared duly elected MP for Northumberland. Having been elected with the backing of the Whigs, Francis voted with them in Parliament. (6)

Having achieved his aim of defeating Douglas, Francis decided he preferred the sea and by 1719 he had returned to the navy. In a letter written on the 26th March he writes: 'the Admiralty have this day given me a commission to command the Gosport, a new 40 gun ship. She is at Deptford and I shall go down next Saturday to put her in commission'. In April he was ordered to sail off the coast of North Britain where he was: 'hereby required and directed to search all ships and vessels that you shall meet with …and in case you find any person on board whom you may have cause to suspect and cannot give a good account of themselves, you are to take them out and secure them till further orders'. This was only four years after the first Jacobite rebellion and there were still many supporters of the old Stuart regime in the region. Francis apparently chased some Spanish ships carrying rebels up to Scotland. In a letter to his father dated 15th May 1719 from Cromarty he writes: 'the rebels with the Spaniards that are landed are but twelve hundred in all as they tell us here, and our forces at Inverness will be as many as they in three or four days'. He also mentioned that as he was sailing up to Scotland: 'I went close under Hartley and fired a gun; but it blew fresh, so that I had no opportunity of sending a boat ashore'. (7)

By June he was back in the North East at Sunderland. It was difficult to recruit sailors for the navy due to the appalling pay and conditions so the navy resorted to very dubious methods to man its ships, often using a press gang to kidnap men and force them to sail in naval ships. The seamen who manned the collier brigs carrying coal to London and the South East were considered excellent seamen and were highly sought after. Fights between seamen and the hated press gangs were common. Francis was ordered by the Admiralty thus: 'am commanded by their Lordships to signify their directions to you that you endeavour to impress as many seafaring men as you can, in the parts where you are... but you are not to take any keelmen'. The keelmen had a monopoly position on the North East rivers. They could control the coal trade and were so powerful that even the navy wouldn't take them on.

Doddington Hall, an Elizabethan mansion built circa 1600.

At the end of June Francis received a letter from the Admiralty ordering him to escort a convoy of ships to the Baltic: 'I am commanded to signify to you their Lordships' directions that you take under your care and protection when you proceed from the Nore to Riga with all such merchant ships as shall be then joined you bound to the aforesaid ports of Reval, Harve, Wybourg and Petersburg and convey them to Riga'. Later in the year he returned to England and in February 1721 we find him in command of His Majesty's Ship Worcester: 'Soon as the said ship shall be fitted at the dock where she is, you are to repair with her to Longreach and there take in your guns and powder, and to furnish her with eight months flesh for the highest complement of men at whole allowances and as much Beer and the Species of dry provisions as she can conveniently store, you are to make the proper application for and get the said provisions on board with all possible expedition'. (7)

This is one of the last letters on naval matters in the Delaval papers. Francis was in London in 1723 when his uncle died and he inherited Delaval Hall. He resigned from the navy to concentrate on sorting out his uncle's affairs including the completion of Delaval Hall. He also had something else to attend to; he was looking for a young heiress to be his wife. For while he had inherited two estates neither produced much income. Fortunately his search was successful and in August 1724, he married Rhoda Apreece, heiress to Doddington Hall in Lincolnshire, in St. Anne's Church in Westminster. She was 21 years old, he was 30.

Rhoda was the daughter of Sarah Hussey and Robert Apreece and although she would inherit a large estate, unfortunately she was not rich. The Hussey family had lived at Doddington for about a hundred years. The hall was built by Thomas Tailor, Registrar to the Bishop of Lincoln in 1600 and designed by Robert Smythson, the great Elizabethan architect. Doddington, which is built of locally made red brick, is considered to be a fine example of his late work.

The Husseys married into the Tailor family and so acquired the estate. During the civil war the family supported the Royalists and after the war ended Cromwell imposed a massive fine on them for supporting the King. This impoverished the family so much that they lived in only a few rooms but they did manage to keep their property. This may have been due to the fact that one of the Hussey daughters married the prominent parliamentarian, General Fairfax. The restoration of the monarchy brought some relief but the house remained sadly neglected until 1760 when Sir John Delaval restored it. (8)

Rhoda inherited the estate on the death of her mother in 1749, her father had died in 1744. Under the terms of the will Doddington was not to be in the same

Ford Castle circa 1760.

ownership as Delaval Hall, this was to prevent it being neglected and becoming a subordinate asset to the Delaval Estate. As we will see this caused family problems later on.

After the wedding Francis wrote to his father saying: 'I am very glad you intend to fix my affairs at Seaton. The first thing you must do after the house is covered will be to lash the floor and seal it, which will I hope be no great expense'. (9) An indication of how much work needed to be done can be gauged from the fact that the attic on the north front is crowned with a pediment containing the arms of Blake, Delaval and Hussey (his wife's family). This could only have been built after Francis inherited the hall. Mewburne, who was supervising the building of Delaval Hall, asked what was to be done next and Francis replied: 'I am resolved to do no more this year than is absolutely necessary to preserve what is already done'. As Delaval Hall wasn't completed until 1728 Francis and Rhoda spent a lot of time in London. In July 1725 he wrote to his father at Dissington: 'wish you joy of a grand daughter. My wife was safely delivered this morning'. (10)

1. *Companion into Northumberland by Sidney Moorhouse, p28, 1953*
   This version of events is disputed. According to Tomlinson, Lady Heron was not at Ford while James was there and it was James who set fire to the castle as he departed. See Comprehensive Guide to the County of Northumberland by W.W. Thomlinson 1910, p520.

2. *On the death of his father, Francis would also inherit the Dissington estate. His father died in 1744 and by 1763 the North Dissington estate had been sold to the Collingwoods who built the present Dissington Hall.*

3. *Ford at the Time of the Waterfords 1822-1907 by James Joicey, p2*

4. *Delaval Papers, p140*

5. *Proceedings of the Society of Antiquaries of Newcastle Third Series Vol. IV 1910, p273*

6. *The House of Commons 1715-1754, by R. Sedgwick, p609*

7. *Letters dealing with naval matters are in the Delaval Papers, p142-149*

8. *Matters concerning Doddington, see R.E.G. Cole, History of the Manor of Doddington, also Doddington Hall, a guide to the house and families that lived there, (no date or author given) and the current guide book by James and Claire Birch.*

9. *Delaval Papers, p14*

10. *ibid p15*

CHAPTER SIX
BODIES IN THE CRYPT

We will take a break from the Delaval story to have a look at the strange story of the body in the crypt. When in 1893 the crypt at the Church of Our Lady was opened up, a lot of bones and rotting coffins were found and six of the coffins had identification plates on them. Two of these plates were removed and are now displayed on the walls in the church, the names on the other coffins were recorded. Of the recorded names four were Delavals and two were not. One of the other names was that of Elizabeth Hicks, she was at one time the young mistress of Sir John (more of her later) so we know why she was there. The other non- Delaval was Sir Alexander Ruthven who died, 3rd January 1722, aged 34. Who was he and why was he buried in the Delaval crypt? (1)

The first place to look was the Delaval family tree but nowhere in these documents is there any mention of a Ruthven. Why would someone who was no relation be buried in the family crypt? The next place to look was in the Earsdon Burial Register (Delaval was part of Earsdon Parish at this time.) and although there is no mention here of a Ruthven being buried in the Church of Our Lady there are records of Delavals being buried around this time. (2)

Where was he staying when he died? As the Delavals buried him we must assume he was staying with them, but not at Delaval Hall as this was only half built so he was probably at Seaton Lodge with Sir John. Also at Seaton Lodge were Sir John's long-standing mistress, a Mrs Poole, and probably his daughter, Anne Rogers, who was married to John Rogers of Denton Hall. Admiral George Delaval was also there at times as he would call there when he came to inspect building progress on Delaval Hall.

Let us now have a look at the Ruthvens, a Scottish family from Rannoch in Perthshire. They feature frequently in the history of Scotland usually up to their necks in mayhem and murder. Patrick, 3rd Lord Ruthven, took a leading part in the murder of Mary Queen of Scots' Italian Secretary, David Rizzio, at Holyrood Palace in 1566. However the 4th Lord Ruthven found favour with the young James VI and was created Earl of Gowrie in 1581. In 1600 John Ruthven 3rd Earl Gowrie and his brother were supposedly involved in a plot to kidnap King James. As a result of the "Gowrie Conspiracy" the brothers were arrested, killed and parts of their bodies were impaled on spikes around Edinburgh! And the peerage was abolished. (3)

The first Ruthven that may be connected to Alexander is a Colonel Sir John Ruthven who served the King of Sweden as a soldier and then became involved in the English Civil War, fighting for the Royalists in the service of King Charles I. He was married twice and died before 1649. His second wife was Barbara Leslie, daughter of Alexander Leslie, First Earl of Leven. Barbara's sister Anne, first married Hugh Fraser, Master of Lovat, and secondly Ralph Delaval in 1646. (4) Thus one could claim there was a vague link through marriage between the Ruthvens and the Delavals. Anne came to live at Seaton and when she died in 1696 she was buried in the crypt at the Church of Our Lady. Where does Alexander fit in to this? He was probably a grandson of Sir John Ruthven and Anne would be an elderly aunt. Sir John was a mercenary soldier fighting for whoever would pay him and it is very likely that Alexander was following family tradition. But what would attract a mercenary soldier to Seaton Sluice in the middle of a cold winter?

A few years earlier, in 1715, the first Jacobite rebellion had occurred. The Jacobites, (from Jacobus, the Latin for James) were supporters of the old Stuart dynasty. They were opposed to the Hanoverian King George I, who became king on the death of Queen Anne in 1714. Many Northumbrian families were Tory or Catholic and opposed to the Whig-Hanoverian government. Northumbrian families who supported the rebels included the Claverings,

Seaton Lodge in Holywell Dene.

38

Widdringtons, Swinburns, Collingwoods and Erringtons. James Radcliffe The 3rd Earl Derwentwater was the nominal leader and was executed in 1716 for his part in the rebellion.

Which side were the Delavals on? Well, they played no part in the 1715 rebellion but this may have been because they saw it, as did many others, as a disorganised shambles and doomed to fail. Opposition to the Hanoverians didn't cease because of the failure in 1715 and plots against the king were frequently exposed by government agents. Were Alexander Ruthven and the Delavals involved in some sort of conspiracy? Sir John Delaval may have been sympathetic to the Jacobites but didn't have the money to employ mercenary soldiers but what about Admiral George? He had money but did he show any sympathy for the Jacobites? There is no written evidence but this is hardly surprising as anything incriminating was destroyed after use, but there is anecdotal evidence suggesting they supported the rebels.

Also, one of the men who took part in the 1715 rebellion was William Shaftoe of Bavington Hall. He was captured, sentenced to death and his estate was seized by the state. William escaped from prison and so saved his life but his estate was sold. Who bought the estate? Well, the estate was bought by Admiral George, and what did he do with it? He gave it to his sister who just happened to be married to William Shaftoe's brother, so the Shaftoe family got their estate back! (5) As a mark of gratitude the Shaftoes frequently used Delaval as a family name. This doesn't prove anything but it does show that an establishment figure, a loyal servant of Queen Anne, could have had sympathy with the Jacobite cause. This brings us back to the fundamental question. What was Sir Alexander Ruthven doing in Seaton Sluice and how did he die on a cold winter's day in 1722? Was he involved in some sort of plot? Who knows? The Delavals left a large archive of papers and letters but there is no mention anywhere of Alexander Ruthven. We only know of him because his coffin was found in the crypt.

This wasn't the only suspicious death at Seaton Lodge. On the very same date, 3rd January, but one year later in 1723 (6) Sir John's daughter, Anne, died. Her death is recorded in the burial register but it doesn't say how she died. Only that she was: ' buried in the chapell of Seaton Delavall in her father's sepulchre the 11th of the said month, January, aged 34 years'. (7) The similarities between their deaths are striking ,both aged 34 years both died on the 3rd January and both buried in the crypt or sepulchre. A further twist is given to Anne's death in that a year after her marriage in 1713, it was reported that she had been poisoned by Sir John's mistress, Mrs Poole, (8) because she had too much influence over her father! Mrs Poole wasn't liked by the rest of the family. Anne didn't die then, but Mrs Poole was present at Seaton Lodge when both she and Ruthven died. Did she do the deed ? Who knows? But we haven't finished with Mrs Poole for when Sir John died in 1729, presumably from natural causes, she tried to seize Seaton Lodge and its effects. Captain Francis Blake Delaval was having none of it, and threats of litigation followed, but eventually the dispute was settled out of court and Francis added Seaton and Hartley to his estate. Meanwhile Mrs Poole accepted a life annuity and left. Would a court hearing have exposed too many dark secrets? And finally what happened to Anne's husband, John Rogers? He went mad! (9)

Notes on chapter six

1. *Church of Our Lady, by Rev G.W. Jackson, Revised 1997, p33*

2, *Earsdon Burial Register, at County Record Office*

3. *The Gowrie Conspiracy, see The Cradle King A life of James V1 &1 by A Stewart 2003, p150*

4. *Email from Mr D.M. Stirling, genealogist and historian*

5. *Strictly speaking he gave it to his nephew thus skipping a generation to avoid further risk of confiscation. A.A. Vol. 12, p223*

6. *Denton Hall and its Associations, by William W. Thomlinson, p47*

7. *See Earsdon Burial Register. In the book on Northumbrian Families, by Percy Hedley, the date of Anne's death is given as 3rd Jan 1722/3 p151. In the Denton Hall book the date of Anne's death is given in the text as 1723 but in the notes on the same page it is given as 1722/3, p46. The burial register is difficult to read. It is just possible that she and Ruthven died at the same time!*

8. *Denton Hall p45*

9. *John Rogers died 24th June, 1758, at his home in Pilgrim Street, Newcastle*

CHAPTER SEVEN
THE GAY DELAVALS

Captain Francis Blake Delaval and his wife Rhoda were able to move in to Delaval Hall in 1728. They proceeded over the next twenty years to have eleven children in a house designed for a bachelor admiral. The first child was a girl, Rhoda, who left a valuable legacy of letters and an heir to the estate. Then came Francis, noted for his wild and debauched ways. John was the second son, solid, hard working on whom the rest of the family came to depend. Then came Thomas, the engineer; Edward the academic, and Robert, George, Henry and Ralph. Two other girls Anne and Sarah lived to become adults.

Although Delaval Hall looks very imposing it was really quite small inside. As the family expanded some of the children went to stay for some time with relatives in other Delaval houses at Dissington and Ford. As the boys grew up they were sent away to Westminster school in London, but only Edward proved to be academically gifted. The girls were given basic education at home learning little more than reading and writing. In the early years their mother, worn out by constant child bearing, let her growing brood slip out of her grasp. Their father was kept busy running the estates so the children grew up to be wild, noisy and undisciplined individuals. However in spite of their preoccupations Francis and Rhoda still found time for pleasure and entertainment and it was around them that the tradition of the fun loving "Gay Delavals" has grown. (1)

A visitor described Seaton Delaval as an: 'Italian Palace and the grounds were a perfect fairyland of light beauty and music'. (2) The Delavals encouraged and welcomed itinerant players and entertainers, references are made to rope-dancers, wire-walkers, and conjurors. A letter from Samuel Foote refers to: 'tournaments, tumbling and bull baiting at Seaton' and also 'two dancing bears' as among the amusements offered by the family. However it wasn't just the well-to-do who were entertained at Delaval Hall. Young Francis invited the local estate workers and farmers to puppet shows, ass races, grinning matches, sack races, and, it is said, even biting the heads off sparrows!

On long winter evenings playing cards was a common pastime and among the Delaval papers some of these old cards have survived. The numbers were printed on one side but the other side was often blank. Some of these blank cards have notes written on them, one of them reads: 'Miss Dalton's Compliments to Mrs. Potter and shall be glad of her company to drink tea with them this afternoon'. (3) This, one of the earliest examples of what became known as visiting cards, was written before April 1750, the year Mrs. Potter married John and so became Mrs. Delaval. When visiting cards became

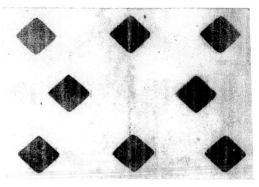

The blank reverse side of playing cards were often used as visiting cards.

fashionable ladies would have their names engraved on special cards and, when paying a call, a lady would first send a footman ahead with her card before descending from her carriage.

Card playing and the gambling that went with it were not however exciting enough for the Delavals and it was to the theatre that they turned for entertainment. With no permanent theatres in the North of England in the first half of the eighteenth century, theatrical entertainment was provided by companies of strolling players. They would move from place to place performing in any large hall they could find, perhaps using a room in an inn or a town hall or a country mansion. They would stay a week or two and then move on. Conditions were very difficult for the actors with no proper changing rooms and as transport was limited they had little scenery and few props.

However the rhetorical style of acting, where the leading actor would come to the front of the stage and proclaim his lines, was easier to produce. During Race Week in Newcastle in 1728, two companies were in town both performing The Beggar's Opera. Did Francis take his wife to see a performance? (4)

As the century progressed the upper classes were not satisfied by the meagre amount of entertainment provide by the strollers and so amateur theatricals became very popular. Many plays were performed at country houses but none were on the scale of those performed by the Delavals at Delaval Hall. The whole family took part in these performances and they would produce tragedies such as Othello or restoration drama such as The Fair Penitent by Nicholas Rowe. This play, one of the most produced plays in the eighteenth century, tells of man's cruelty to women and is noted for its rebellious and outspoken female protagonist Calista. Part of one of her speeches reads: -

"How hard is the condition of our sex,

Thro'ev'ry state of life the slaves of men!"(5)

However not everything was as serious as this. In 1753, at Christmas, they produced a pantomime written by Robert Delaval which included 'rope dancers, wire walkers,and conjurors'. The pantomime was performed 'before a great number of country people who showed their approbation by great fits of laughter'. (6) It was young Francis who often took the lead in these productions. He seemed to be obsessed by the theatre and, as we shall see, he had some very dubious actor friends. His stationer's bill for 1737 includes such items as: 'binding a parcel of play 9d, for the Tragedy of King Charles 1,1s, for Jane Grey, Henry VIII, The Indian Queen, 3 plays 1s 6d'. (7) The audience for these plays would have been other members of the family, servants, local gentry and often the local inhabitants as play bills have been preserved advertising and inviting people to attend. The play was usually performed in the entrance hall but if there was a large audience it could only have been held outside. The north front steps and courtyard would have provided a wonderful backdrop and setting. (8)

The Delavals knew how to entertain on a grand scale. After a performance of The Fair Penitent in 1792 the expenses came to over £66. There was a huge amount of food including: 'ornamental swan and boar's heads, 12 lobsters, 50 raspberry tarts, 25 plates of figs.' And for the animals that brought the guests: 'hay for 80 horses'. The bill for ales, wines and spirits was over £17. Extra staff were taken on in the kitchen and: '2 fiddlers for the dance after supper.' (9) Nor did the Delavals confine themselves to performing at Delaval Hall. On more than one occasion they used London theatres to put on plays in which they took leading acting parts. As the century progressed theatres were built in the north of England. In 1764 a Mr. Bates opened a theatre in North Shields and by 1789 this theatre was being managed by a Mr. Cawdell who put on a new play The Battle of Hexham. The Newcastle Chronicle, of 5th December informs us that the Right Hon. Lord Delaval attended the performance. In 1791 Mr. Cawdell built a theatre in South Shields financed by public subscription and the list of subscribers was headed by Lord Delaval. (10)

Many stories are told of extraordinary goings-on at Delaval Hall. Crowds of visitors gathered there; fun and laughter filled the rooms; all sorts of entertainments took place. The gardens glowed with candle light and music and guests abandoned themselves to merriment and pleasure. Practical jokes were all part of the fun and at this the Delaval boys were past masters. Going to bed at Delaval Hall could be a very traumatic experience. Guests would retire to their bedrooms and after a few minutes, while they were undressing, mechanical hoists would raise the bedroom walls exposing them in complete disarray. In one bedroom there was a four-poster bed which could be lowered into a bath of cold water, complete with occupants, by winding a handle in the room next door. In another room the drunken guest, (that was most of them!), would be put to bed in the dark, and awaken in the morning to find himself apparently lying on the ceiling. The room was completely inverted, the chairs and tables were stuck to the ceiling, and the chandelier was in the middle of the floor! Not the best way to start the day especially with a blinding hangover. Other bedtime pranks included putting ducks and geese in beds and hiding mannequins of old Delavals in wardrobes. One guest was put to bed in a room with the windows blacked out and slept all through the next day and the next….

Shortly after the new stables were completed around 1765, Francis invited the local gentry to a banquet at the Hall. When they arrived they found the place deserted and in darkness. Confused and irritated they were about to leave when the doors to the new stables were thrown open to reveal a superb feast set out around the new horse boxes. However the guests sometimes got their own back. Francis boasted he could walk through the gardens blindfolded but he cheated by carefully laying out a thin thread which he would pick up and follow. Someone spotted this and carefully moved the thread over one of the lily ponds!

Staying at Delaval Hall could be unpleasant for other reasons. Lord Strathmore commented: 'Sir John's (Vanburgh) general plan was to enter the building direct from the north into a magnificent hall with a corridor leading left to right, the consequence was that the current of air from the exterior was unchecked and rendered the building in cold weather almost uninhabitable.' (11) Strathmore complained at the lack of comfort in the house and always took an extra cloak when staying there. Other guests complained about the food. It appears that they mainly ate lamb or mutton and this was often cold as the kitchens were in the west wing and the food had to be carried down draughty corridors before it reached the dining room. Staying at Delaval Hall might be uncomfortable but never dull!

Notes on Chapter Seven

1. *The Gay Delavals, by Francis Askham Francis and Rhoda were not the first fun loving Delavals, an entry in some accounts listed on p124 of The Delaval Papers reads: 'July 18th 1723 Paid for the Fools Coat 00 08 06'.*

2. *Delaval Hall guide book, p19*

3. *Delaval Papers, p194*

4. *Archaelogia Aeliania, Third Series Vol. XI The Northern Stage. p56*

5. *The Fair Penitent, 1791 edition*

6. *Delaval Papers, p84*

7. *ibid p85*

8. *For the 1791 production the theatre was in the entrance hall and 100 guests were seated. The Courts of Europe, Swinburne 1841, p99*

9. *Delaval Papers, p93*

10. *North Shields Theatres, by R. King, p31*

11. *Delaval Papers, p127*

CHAPTER EIGHT
RHODA 1725-1757

Rhoda was the first child of Captain Francis Blake Delaval and Rhoda Apreece. We know very little about her early life but in 1751 she married Edward Astley of Melton Constable in Norfolk. Like most of the Delaval girls Rhoda was noted for her good looks and talent. She was an accomplished composer and artist, and left some fine paintings, including a charming self portrait.

She also left a good selection of letters written in the years after her marriage which are charming, full of family gossip and littered with medical advice. There are also some references to a lottery draw. The eighteenth century version had a top prize of £10,000. Tickets were expensive so poor people would buy shares in a ticket. These letters offer a fascinating insight into society life in eighteenth century Northumberland.

This first letter was written shortly after her marriage from her husband's home in Melton, to Mrs Delaval (her brother John's wife, Susanna) in Albemarle Street, London : 'It gives me the greatest joy imaginable to hear, my dear sister, that you are so much better than when I left you. Tell my brother that I am infinitely obliged to him for his letter. I shall be vastly happy when we meet altogether at Doddington. You cannot imagine what a continual hurry we live in here. What with going out and company coming I have hardly an hour to myself. Today Lord and Lady Buckingham, and Lady Dorothy and Sir William and Lady Harbart, and I know not who else, dines here. Mr Astley begs to be remembered to you and my brother in the kindest manner. The hearing a good account of your health gave him sincere pleasure. We are to go on Monday to stay with his Aunt Stileman, seventy miles from here. Miss Astley goes with us. In the way thither I shall see my Lord Oxford and my Lord Leicester. I have a thousand compliments and good wishes to you and the family here. I am afraid I shall not be dressed for dinner if I do not begin, therefore must conclude.

Yours most affectionately R Astley.'

As you can see they led a busy social life. In the following letter from Seaton Delaval she gives a liberal amount of medical advice.

'My Dear Sister, I am quite of Spence' opinion in thinking that moderate Diet is the best thing for you; nor can I think that Scarborough would be any service in your case. I hope you take the air in the coach each day; it is much better than walking even when you are able. I wish you had some one to stay with you.

The elder children of Rhoda and Francis Blake Delaval by Sir Arthur Pond. Young Rhoda with her brothers Francis, John and Thomas. (Courtesy: Doddington Hall).

It would not be much confinement to my brother, tho' I dare say he thinks it none, and I hear he is the best nurse in the world. Pray did Mr. Harton's friend recover that took Dr James's medicine? I have intended to ask you every time I write. Poor Long Jack is so ill of a fever that they think he cannot live. My mother sent him some of Dr James's medicine. Whether they gave it him in a proper manner I can't tell; but I am afraid it will not have the proper effect. Poor Sir John-the vanities of this life are all over with him now. While he was well he appeared every Sunday at church in his fine clothes and long wig and sword. The first time the country people came out of their seats to make room for so fine a gentleman; but you may imagine what a laugh ensued when they found out the jay in borrowed plumes.' Long Jack was an old and trusted Delaval servant and 'Sir John' was an affectionate title the family sometimes gave him. Rhoda then goes on to discuss the lottery: 'My brother Ned bids me tell you he intends to send immediately for a Ticket. He is convinced you or he must have the ten thousand pounds-everyone for themselves. We hope not. My father has promised Bob one, which you may imagine is no small pleasure to him.'

The social scene was very important to her and we get a glimpse of it here: 'Mrs Charlton is gone home' (to Hesleyside in north Northumberland). ' We saw her often while she was in this part of the country; she looks in high beauty this year. Tinemouth and Cullercoats were much in fashion not a room empty. My Lady Ravensworth and my Lady Clavering were a month at Cullercoats bathing. My Lady Clavering and Sir Thomas dined here the other day.' Just before she finishes the letter she says: ' I am just now told Long Jack has had a good night and is in a fair way of doing well. What a fine thing Dr James' s powder is. Pray let me hear from you very soon.'

In this next letter, we see the Delavals mixing with the best of Newcastle society. Rhoda writes: 'My Dear Sister, Yesterday night we were all of us at Newcastle Assembly. There was a great deal of good company. It was the day of the Mayor's Feast. Ridley is Mayor. My Lady Blackett was there, and made many enquiries after you. My Lord Ravensworth dined here the other day.' This letter is undated but we can date it as 1751 because that is when Matthew Ridley was Mayor of Newcastle.

She continues with one of her favourite topics: 'It is surprising what great cures have been done by Dr James's Powder, here a very sad fever has gone round the country; all who have taken it (the powder) have recovered. I believed I told you that Sir John is quite well, and seven more at Hartley that have taken the powders, after they had been light headed for some days.' John Robinson who collected the Delaval Papers in 1880 says that the people of Hartley still use Dr James's powder! Rhoda concludes her letter with more mundane topics: 'I'm sorry your turnips have not turned out so well as they should have done; but it has been a very bad season. About this place they have had a fine harvest.' And finally she asks: ' Do you intend going to London this year?'

I'm sure many of us will be familiar with the sentiments expressed in this letter, written to Mrs Delaval at Doddington, concerning the lottery: 'Poor me! All my golden hopes are come to nothing, for my ticket, that was to have been ten thousand pounds, is come up a blank. I hope to hear that you had better luck.'

And another familiar moan: 'This place affords no news. The weather has been so bad for sometime we have seen no creatures.'

It is from a letter written in May, 1752 that we learn of the damage done by a fire to the west wing of Delaval Hall: 'My Dear Sister, You desire an account of the damage the fire has done, and how it happened. About twelve years ago a man undertook to prevent the chimney from smoking. He pared away the wall at the back of the chimney till he came to one of the beams and was so great a villain as never to mention it. It is very surprising how it escaped so long without being burnt. It was first seen by my maid when she went up after dinner. She called out for help. My Father who was in the passage immediately went up and saw the fire breaking out. He alarmed all the workman, and in less than a quarter of an hour, four hundred people were gather'd together. They, by pulling down and throwing great quantities of water, saved the kitchen and all beyond it. The fire burnt with such swiftness that it was impossible to save any of our linnin , or indeed hardly anything that was in those two rooms next to the kitchen.'

The Delavals were lucky this time as the fire was quickly found and put out without too much damage. They would not be so lucky in 1822! Fire was a big problem in these large houses which were lit by candles, warmed by open fires, and had rooms which were furnished with wooden furniture and large tapestries. In the years before there was a proper fire service, many houses were damaged or destroyed by fires.

Sea bathing and taking the waters was becoming fashionable and it is interesting to see Rhoda's comments about two local seaside resorts which were little more than villages until bathing became popular with the upper classes. She writes to her sister: 'Mrs. Charlton is at Cullercoats bathing. They tell me it is much the fashion this year, that there is a good deal of company there and at Tynemouth. This place is in high beauty. If you should be tempted to see it don't leave your little girl behind whatever you do; the change of air will do her as much good as you.'

This last letter written at Seaton is, like the other letters, addressed to Mrs Delaval at Doddington. This Mrs. Delaval is really her brother John's wife, Susanna. 'My Dear Sister, It is true that I have not been well for sometime, and I am grown much thinner than when you last saw me. I sent for Dr. Cooper who says that if what he prescribes besides asses milk and spa water, which I drink together in the morning, has not had the proper effect I must go to Tunbridge in June.' (1) This letter is dated 14th April but there is no year given, however as it refers to her ill health it was probably written in 1757 the year that she died.

Rhoda took Dr. Cooper's advice and went south for the summer, but it didn't save her life. She died in the October while staying with friends at Bath. When she died, probably as result of complications in childbirth, she was only 32. Her first son had died soon after his birth in 1755, her second son Jacob was born at Delaval Hall in September, 1756, and she died shortly after the birth of her third son, Francis, who survived. Rhoda's death was a sad loss to the Delavals, for after her father's death in 1752, she had virtually run Delaval Hall rather than her mother who had withdrawn from much of the daily routine. Rhoda is buried at Widcombe parish church near Bath, close to the house where she died.

After her death, her husband went to live with his children at his family home in Melton Constable, Norfolk. He died in 1802 aged 73. His surviving son Jacob inherited the Delaval Estates in 1814. Francis, his other son, was a naval officer who was killed on the Saucy Arethusa in her famous fight with the French frigate La Belle Poule in 1778. (2)

Notes on Chapter eight.

1. The Letters quoted in this chapter are all in the Delaval Papers, p 58-68.

2. Information about the Astley Family is taken from an unpublished booklet compiled by the family dated 1936.

CHAPTER NINE
SIR FRANCIS BLAKE DELAVAL
MP and RAKE

Captain Francis Blake Delaval managed his various estates to maintain his life-style but he did little to improve them and, with the exception of filling the office of High Sheriff in 1730, he took no further part in the public life of the county. He had the misfortune to fall from his horse in December, 1752, he broke his leg and died shortly afterwards. He was buried in the Church of Our Lady where his coffin plate is now on display. His eldest son, Francis, showed little interest in anything except enjoying himself. It was John and Thomas who later developed the estate to its full potential.

Francis was the person behind many of the practical jokes which plagued visitors to Delaval Hall, but his first love was the theatre and acting. Tall with fair complexion and light hair, he was attractive and had been well educated at public school and Oxford, but he never showed much interest in work. The rest of the family soon recognised this and so he was persuaded to let John take over many of the responsibilities of the eldest son in return for an annual allowance. His father hoped he would become an MP and he was persuaded to fight a by-election but failed to win the seat.

Now turned twenty, Francis was bored with life at Seaton. He wanted more than the limited social life of country sports and horses and was spending an increasing amount of time in London lured by the temptations of city life and the prospect of theatrical entertainment. Horace Walpole in one of his letters mentions that: 'Delaval, a wild young fellow, keeps an Italian woman, called the Tedeschi.' She was presumably Caterina Tedeschi, a Venetian opera singer. Walpole goes on to describe how Francis caught her in bed with a handsome young eunuch, dragged the lovers out of bed and horsewhipped them. (1) It had not taken very long for Francis to be noticed by the gossip writers of the day. While Francis was away two young ladies came to Delaval Hall. One was his cousin Susanna Potter. Her husband, John Potter, the Under Secretary of State for Ireland, had died suddenly. Susanna, then aged about twenty, was the daughter of Margaret Robinson (nee Delaval), the Captain's sister.

The other young lady, Betty Roach, was aged about nineteen and was Mr Potter's ward. He had become the legal guardian of Betty and her sister, Deodata, about six months before his death. He may have taken in these two unfortunate teenage girls as companions for his young wife. Betty and her sister, the illegitimate daughters of Major Roach and a Mrs Raworth, were born and brought up in India. Major Roach intended to retire to England and he sent his young daughters, then aged about nine and ten, and their mother back to England before him. It was two years before Major Roach returned to England only to find that their mother appeared to have rejected the girls and she didn't want him. The girls were boarded out to various people and they eventually finished up at a Catholic convent school in Paris. Major Roach died shortly afterwards, leaving a small legacy to the girls but nothing for their mother.

The inheritance was to be paid to the girls when they were twenty one or on marriage. When the girls were in their late teens they returned to London and a legal battle ensued between the trustees appointed by their late father and Mrs Raworth. In the Court of Chancery the guardianship of the girls was hotly debated. The trustees arguing that the girls' mother was totally unsuitable to look after their interest and was scheming to get her hands on their legacy. The girls made it clear that they wanted nothing to do with their mother, indeed Deodata threatened to stab her if she interfered with them. The case became notorious and the plight of the girls aroused much sympathy. The girls needed a legal guardian until they reached their majority and this is where Mr Potter entered the story. Moved by their plight he agreed to look after them but, sadly for everyone, he died shortly afterwards. Deodata slipped away to make her own life in London while Betty and Susanna made that fateful journey to Seaton Delaval.

At Seaton they were made welcome, especially by John who was much taken by his cousin. Francis was in London when they came to Seaton but he may have met Betty in London. It was when he returned to Seaton that he began seducing this poor, unfortunate, vulnerable young girl. She was quite unable to resist Francis and soon she was captivated. He amused himself with her for a while and then feeling the hostility of the family and bored with Seaton, he returned to London. With Francis gone Seaton lost its appeal for Betty and Captain Francis and Rhoda turned against her. She hoped to marry Francis but they wanted more than a poor low class, illegitimate girl to marry the heir to Delaval Estates. So Betty left Seaton and followed Francis to London where she became his long-term mistress. He had no intention of marrying her, but over the next few years, she bore him two illegitimate children. The first was a boy, called Francis, afterwards known as Frank, and the second was a girl called Frances, and known as Fanny. Betty wanted everyone to know who was the father of her children! (2)

The Delavals, like most wealthy families had property in London. Captain Francis Blake Delaval had taken a house in 1738 on what is now the site of 12

Downing Street, and the family kept the house until 1758. In 1762 Sir Francis Blake Delaval took the lease on a house on the site of number 11 Downing Street. The rate book shows the previous tenant as Sir Edward Astley. At this time Downing Street had a rural aspect as it backed onto parkland but it was also convenient for the city. It was just a short walk away from Russell Street. It was at Tom's Coffee House on Russell Street that Francis fell in with a bunch of dissolute actors led by Samuel Foote. (2A)

Foote was about seven years older than Delaval. He came from a prosperous Cornish family, was well educated, and like Delaval, he went to Oxford, had inherited money, yet lived way above his income. He deserted his wife and loved the theatre.

He soon gave up an early career as a barrister and put his talent for oratory, mimicry and wit to use by becoming an actor. He became well known for writing and performing one man shows at the Little Theatre in Haymarket doing satirical sketches about the great and the good, much to the delight of his unruly audience.

Nothing new and no-one famous or fashionable escaped his wit. Gentlemen of fashion visited Foote's Green Room and here Delaval met people like David Garrick, manager of the Drury Lane Theatre, and Charles Macklin, Foote's actor friend. (3)

Francis mixed with London Society and enjoyed an idle lifestyle. A gentleman, on a typical day in London, would get up around 10 or 11 am, venture into the city, visit a coffee house for the latest political gossip and read the daily papers. In the afternoon if it was fine he might take a walk in the park or if it was wet he might stay in the coffee house playing cards and gambling. He would take dinner in the late afternoon and then go to a theatre or club. Later he would meet friends in a tavern and drink and gamble with dice or cards into the small hours.

The London theatres were not as exciting as might be supposed. Since 1737, the Lord Chamberlain had the power to censor plays so few risks were taken; sentimental comedies abounded but at Drury Lane David Garrick did revive Shakespeare. Garrick insisted on rehearsals, got rid of inherited parts and banned spectators from the stage. But he caused a riot when he tried to stop half price admission for those who arrived after the interval only to see and be seen.

Life in London was not always pleasant. Many of the older streets were unpaved and those that were paved were often covered in horse manure and mud. As the rich and poor lived almost next to each other, the atmosphere was volatile.

Violence was commonplace. Thieves and pickpockets were everywhere, drunks slumped in doorways and whores plied their trade. Nocturnal travel was hazardous even if you were helped by link boys who, for pennies, would light your way with fire brands. Gas lighting was not introduced until 1809 when Piccadilly was the first street to be lit by gas.

However fashionable squares were multiplying, their gardens closed to the common people. Hyde Park was also privileged territory with deer being there till 1768. Here on summer evenings the gentry would parade in their carriages in order to be seen. The rule of the road was simple. At a junction the person of highest rank took precedent. Francis once bet that he would make the Duke of Somerset give way to him. None of the nobility would give way to a scoundrel like Delaval so he cheated. He painted his carriage with the livery of the Duke of Norfolk so naturally Somerset gave way! (4) However Francis had a problem. His extravagant life style could not be met by his modest income and he was in debt.

Now Samuel Foote, also in debt, decided the solution to their problems was for Francis to marry a wife - a rich one! Francis was happy to go along with his idea. Foote had come across a rich widow, Lady Isabella, widow of Lord Nassau Paulet, and although she was about sixty and going senile, she was reputed to have a £100,000 fortune and had indicated to Foote that she was interested in getting married again. Isabella was the daughter of Thomas 6th Earl of Thanet. When he died the title passed to his cousin but his estate went to his five daughters of which Isabella was the youngest. To persuade Lady Isabella to marry Francis Delaval, Foote dreamt up an elaborate charade. He told her he knew of an extraordinary man who could foretell future events such as marriage. There was a 'genuine' fortune teller who had a good reputation near the Old Bailey and Foote offered to take her to see him. Isabelle agreed to go and seek his advice. Foote then hired a room a few doors away from the fortune teller and bribed one of his acting friends, Jemmy Worsdale, to dress up and play the role of the fortune teller. Lady Isabella swallowed the bait and a few days later she was taken by Samuel Foote to meet his fortune teller. Jemmy, disguised with a long white beard, and wearing a turban and star-studded cloak, had been suitably coached and he told Isabella all sorts of private things about herself. He then told her she would meet the man she would marry if she went to Green Park the next Thursday where she would observe: 'a tall fair gentleman, remarkably handsome, dressed in blue and silver.' (5) She went to Green Park and there of course was Delaval dressed exactly as described. Within a few days they were married. On 8th March 1750, the fat, elderly Isabella left St George's Chapel, Hanover Square, as the bride of Francis Delaval. Unfortunately for him, her fortune was not £100,000 but more like £24,000 of which £12,000 was pledged to Foote as his pay off! Whether any of the family attended the wedding is not recorded, but Lady Isabella appears to have visited Seaton in 1751, as Rhoda notes in a letter written at Seaton - "Lady Isabella set out for London today." No mention is made of Francis.

To celebrate, if that's the right word, Francis spent £1,500 to hire Drury Lane Theatre and in March, 1752, the Delavals put on Othello and all the family played parts. Francis played Othello, John was Iago, Thomas played Cassio and Betty was Desdemona. A chronicler at the time wrote: 'Tickets were delivered to as many as could conveniently fill the house, without specifying any particular part, so that the shilling gallery was as much crowded with nobility as the boxes; stars shone among the gods, and ribbons were peeping out of the slips. The House of Commons adjourned two hours earlier than usual to enable members to be present; the streets were crowded by carriages, that the greatest part of the audience…quitted their coaches at a great distance and were seen walking full dressed through the crowd. In a word, it was the most splendid appearance of nobility ever seen in a theatre and including Royalty itself; and so anxious were the polite world to be present that ten guineas was offered and refused for a ticket.' (6) Those who attended included their Royal Highnesses, the Prince and Princess of Wales, The Duke of Cumberland, Princess Amelia, Prince George and Princess Augusta. In the Green Room after the performance, Foote was heard to remark that he had never felt so sorry for anyone in his life. When asked who he was referring to he replied: 'For Shakespeare, of course.' (7)

Francis was still keen to become a member of parliament and in 1751 a by-election occurred at the small Wiltshire borough of Hindon. No doubt using some of Isabella's money, he went to Hindon and convinced the electorate that he was the best person to look after their interests. He was duly elected and became their M.P.

In December 1752, his father died and he inherited the estates at Seaton, Hartley, Ford and Horton. However Francis was quite incapable of managing them and within three years he was in debt to the tune of £45,000. A private Act of Parliament was obtained for the payment of his debts by sale or mortgage of his estates. The manors of Ford, Horton and Hartley were vested in John Delaval and Elisha Biscoe, who were empowered as trustees to raise the sum of £45,000 by mortgaging the Ford Estate. Francis retained the management of Seaton Delaval and was paid an annuity of £4,000 a year. This meant that Francis gave up most of his inheritance in return for the annuity, and John, who was far more capable, got his hands on the estates. (8) When Rhoda's mother died she made sure, with a clause in her will, that the Doddington Estates could not be held by the person holding the Seaton Estate. She knew this would stop Francis, who she never liked, getting his hands on Doddington which was left to the second in line, John. Whatever his financial state, Francis could never resist playing the fool. Within months of his father's death, four thousand people were said to have watched fire eaters, rope walkers and conjurors performing at Delaval Hall.

By 1754 the electors of Hindon had had enough of Francis and he was forced to look for a new seat. At the general election in that year he stood as candidate at the Hampshire town of Andover. The electors were delighted by his lavish hospitality, charmed by his smooth tongue and bought on nomination day when he fired a cannon filled with 500 golden guineas across the town square. Bribing the electors was nothing new. Most winning candidates resorted to it, but only Francis did it so dramatically. Once elected he did little work as an MP. He was more likely to be seen in a box at Covent Garden than on the benches in the House of Commons; but one advantage of being an M.P. was that you could claim parliamentary privilege and so avoid being sent to jail for being in debt.

Although known for being wild and sensation-seeking, he also showed an interest in scientific developments and collected scientific instruments and novelties. In his house on Downing Street, he had steam engines, 'orreries' - model monkeys that ran up and down sticks – and he collected toys and novelties of all kinds. According to the Memoirs of Richard Edgeworth: 'The ingenuity of some of the contrivances attracted the notice not only of those who sort amusement but also men of letters and science' (9). It was because of his interests in such things and his wild reputation that Francis always had a place in the coffee house circuit, and it was here that he met His Royal Highness, Prince Edward Augustus, brother of Prince George, later King George III. The Prince was described by the Duchess of Northumberland as: 'remarkably plain but with a mind so devoted to pleasure and so little regard to propriety as robb'd him of his Dignity and made him rather a trifling than an amiable Character' (10) A social butterfly he flitted from one event to another. Francis was as at ease with the aristocratic prince as he was with Foote and his actor friends.

By 1758 Francis was again in debt and neither the glamour of the Prince's circle nor his acting friends could cure his boredom. He then astonished everyone by enlisting in the army. In 1756 Britain had yet again gone to war with the French in what became known as The Seven Years War. Francis found himself part of an expeditionary force, under the command of Sir Richard Howe, ordered to attack the Brittany coast at St Malo. Francis was part of a company of

Grenadiers. As the fleet prepared to land on the beach Francis leapt over board and invaded France alone. There was, fortunately for Francis, no opposition to the landing and for a time he was the hero of the hour. For being the first Grenadier to storm the beach he was awarded a knighthood!

Francis had no intention of staying in the army and a few weeks later he was back in London dining out on the story. His fame was such that it was said of him, that together with Prince Fredrick of Brunswick and Mr Pitt he was: 'The most fashionable man in England.' (11)

If the marriage of Sir Francis to Lady Isabella can be said to have begun as a farce it ended in acrimony. Francis began the expensive and lengthy proceedings to divorce Isabella on the grounds of adultery within months of the marriage. To the delight of the popular press the Paulet family counter-sued Francis on the grounds of his adultery with Betty Roach. The trial took place in January 1755. The press published the sordid details of the case and Georgian London gossiped about the scandalous behaviour of the upper classes. The trial documents consist mainly of witness statements. The witnesses included the friends and servants of the accused. The Paulet family lawyers subpoenaed Francis's servants. (11A)

Francis's lawyers dragged Lady Isabella's name through the courts and produced witnesses of her liaisons with other men. Servants' eyewitness reports are always problematic for they knew who paid their wages and good jobs were hard to come by. On the other hand, resentful servants may betray their employer while loyal retainers are faithful to the end and swear they saw nothing. It is hardly surprising that witnesses often contradict one another. Among the witness statements produced at the trial are those of James Dupree who was an old friend of Samuel Foote. Dupree met up with Samuel, Francis, Paul Saunders and John Shaw at The Cardigan's Head. Here Francis talked of his wife's infidelities at Haddock's Bagnio, a notorious "bath" house. His friends volunteered to go and spy on Isabella, so that night, around midnight, Saunders and Shaw went to Haddocks Bagnio and later swore that they had rushed in to a room and seen Isabella in bed with a strange man. You might think that would settle the case but their evidence was thrown out on the not unreasonable grounds that they were both drunk at the time. The case brought by Lady Isabella against Francis was dismissed despite the fact that Betty Roach had two children by Francis. The law treated women very harshly in the 18th century. After the court case Lady Isabella dropped out of Francis's life. She died in 1763 in obscurity. When Francis recovered from the drama of the court case and the excitement of his brief military career he resumed his political interests.

In 1761 Francis went back to Andover to defend his parliamentary seat, employing his unique electioneering style, a mix of bribery and charm. In conversation with one reluctant elector he discovered that the man had never seen a fire-eater so he promptly summoned the famous Angelo down from London to give a demonstration which secured the man's vote. His agent's election expenses even include a £500 surgeon's bill for mending a broken leg.

Trying to imitate the pranks of Francis the agent had invited the Mayor and Corporation and the officers from the local regiment to dinner and drinks on the King's birthday at The George Inn, Andover. Each thought the other group was paying and when they discovered they had been duped, the agent was thrown out of the window - hence the broken leg. Francis was returned as MP for Andover but he lost the seat in 1765. (12)

Two and a half years after his military exploits, Francis went to Westminster Abbey to be installed with due pomp and ceremony as a Knight Companion of the Most Honourable Military Order of the Bath. He was described as: 'One of the finest figures of all the Knights.' (13)

When London proved too constricting Francis might go back to Seaton for a while or to Cannons, the country house in Middlesex where his sister, Sarah and her husband, the Earl of Mexborough, lived. Samuel Foote and Prince Edward were also frequent visitors there.

They put on plays and entertainments mixing drama with puppet shows, grinning matches and sack races where aristocratic guests were made to hop their way to victory. It was while they were at Cannons rehearsing the play, The Fair Penitent, that Foote broke his leg. Perhaps as a result of goading by Prince Edward and others, Foote was unwisely persuaded to ride a spirited horse. He was thrown off the horse and broke his leg so badly it had to amputated. Full of remorse Prince Edward did his best to help.

As Foote explained in a letter to John Delaval: 'I took the liberty to mention to his Royal Highness that a patent from the Crown for the House in the Haymarket would protect me from want'. (14) Thanks to the influence of Prince Edward he got a licence to put on plays from May to September and in 1767 Foote bought the Little Theatre outright and renamed it, the Theatre Royal.

Meanwhile Francis had requested Richard Edgeworth to fit out his own private theatre in St. James Street, Westminster. While the theatre was being prepared Francis and Prince Edward paid visits to Newmarket flirting with a string of women. By October 1766 the theatre was ready to stage The Fair Penitent. The family again took part. Francis played Horatio, Calista was admirably acted by

Lady Stanhope, Lady Mexborough played Lavinia, John played Sciolto and Prince Edward, now Duke of York, played the hero and seducer Lothario, much to Lady Mary's alarm as she thought it was so unbecoming to royal dignity. 'I was concern'd the Duke shou'd do anything so contrary to decorum' she noted in her diary.. Thomas Gray in a letter dated May 1767 refers to the Duke of York as Manager of the theatre. The one-legged Foote, on this occasion, did not take part. In December 1766, The Earl of March told his friend George Selwyn that he had been passing his time: 'chiefly with his Royal Highness, the Chavalier Delaval and the Opera people' adding 'we live very high'. (15)

In May 1763 Francis went to Covent Garden to see Comus by Milton. This was a masque in honour of chastity and playing the role of the nymph, Sabrina, was a young Ann Catley. Francis was captivated by her. He made himself known to her and uncovered details of her private life. She was the daughter of a coachman and was apprenticed to a Mr. Bates, a musician who was training her to sing. Francis found out that neither Bates nor Ann were happy with the arrangement, so he had a lawyer draw up new indentures in which he agreed to teach her in the art of music on condition she would stay in his house. Francis paid off Bates and Ann came to live with him. Soon they were seen out riding together in Hyde Park and it became obvious that Francis was teaching her more than singing. When her father discovered her change of circumstances he was horrified. He thought Francis would lead his daughter into prostitution and he sued Francis for debauching his daughter. The judge gave his full sympathy to the obviously pregnant Ann, who had been ill treated by her father, bullied by Bates and debauched by Francis Blake Delaval. The judge said Francis: 'has in the whole affair acted very ill and very unwisely'. (16) He fined Francis, awarded costs against him and discharged Ann from his care. Whereupon her father rushed forward to drag her out of court. The judge reprimanded him and Ann left court arm in arm with Francis!

To cool the inevitable scandal, Francis decided to send Ann to Dublin in the care of Foote's actor friend, Charles Macklin, who was appearing at the New Dublin Theatre. Ann was soon appearing on the Dublin stage where she enjoyed great success and when she returned to London she soon worked her way into Prince Edward's inner circle. Years later when she came to write her memoirs she claimed to have had two illegitimate children, one by Delaval the other by Prince Edward. (17)

The stables in the East Wing of Delaval Hall.

Meanwhile, what had happened to Betty? Well she had not sat at home waiting for Francis to call. His lack of money meant that Betty was not adequately provided for so she wrote to John asking for help pointing out that her debts were part of Francis's and should have been cleared when his were. John agreed and paid them.

In 1758 she went to Edinburgh and married an eighteen year old Irish Baronet, Sir Henry Echlin. In 1762 she married him again, in Dublin! Apparently she was not happy that the first marriage was legal. However she did not stay with him for long. She left him and returned to London perhaps because she heard of Lady Isabella's death. Any hopes she may have had about marrying Francis were soon dashed. He had no intention of giving up his dissolute life and settling down with Betty. With no sign of her Irish husband Betty, the deserted mistress, was shunned by society and lived a bitter and lonely life with just young Frank for company although he, and especially Fanny, spent a lot of time with the Mexboroughs at Cannon Park.

While Francis spent most of his time in London he did make frequent visits to Seaton where he kept a pack of hounds and would go hunting on foot or by horse. Fox hunting was not yet the dominant sport it became and the quarry was often the hare. In his youth Francis was a good horseman but as he grew older his weight became a problem. In 1765 Francis spent some time at Seaton Delaval while he rebuilt the stable block. He wrote to his brother John: ' I am putting up the grand stable on a plan we saw at Lord Hoptoun's with stone divisions of the stalls which I am sure you will like as they are very agreeable to the rest of the building'. (18) The stables are still there, a monument to Francis; frivolous, extravagant but rather grand.

As Francis's financial position got worse he borrowed money from friends and family. In 1769, his sister Sarah (Mexborough) lent him £10,000 but by 1770 the money had gone, so humbled and near bankrupt he met John at Doddington where he sold out completely giving up Delaval Hall and estates in return for an annuity of £4,000 a year. Francis produced his long list of creditors including the Mexboroughs and the proprietor of White's Club. John refused to pay his debts but said they should be a charge upon the estate.

Francis gave up his house in Downing Street and went to live at the Mexborough's house in Dover Street. Francis had no assets so it is probable that he had gambled his money away.

This was at a time when at White's Club, of which Francis was a member, Lord Arlington could bet £30,000 on which of two raindrops trickling down a window pane would reach the bottom first! Edgeworth notes: 'He (Francis) had a universal acquaintance with all the gay and all the gambling world'. (19) On another occasion he relates that Francis put a £500 bet on the result of a race between two equally matched horses at Newmarket. Francis along with others, considered setting up a system based on the newly invented Telegraph, to get the results of horse races before the horse courier arrived with the official result but the system proved too complicated to set up.

When his friend Prince Edward died suddenly, in September, 1767 Francis was deeply upset. He seemed to shrivel and lose hope and his spirit and health deteriorated. His sister, the recently divorced Lady Stanhope, had been having an affair with the Prince and Francis had hoped that it would lead to their marriage. His lifestyle did nothing for his health and he became grossly fat but it was alcohol and late nights which finally sapped his strength. On the 7th August 1771 after a huge meal he collapsed and died at the age of 44. He was alone except for his manservant and within hours his creditors were besieging the house. As soon as his body was taken from Dover Street for burial at Seaton, his funeral became a public spectacle. Before and behind the hearse, which was drawn by a team of six horses was a coach and six horses manned by men in black. It took three weeks to reach Seaton.

The elegant portico on the south front of the Hall.

In every large town where the cortege stopped, his coffin lay in state in a room at the best inn. At Newcastle a further twenty-one horsemen joined the procession to Seaton and the Church of Our Lady, where, with due ceremony, Francis was finally laid to rest - the last Delaval to be buried in the family church. So eager were all classes to see the event that in the rush a girl had her leg broken and many people had their clothes torn and their pockets picked. The undertaker's bill came to £690. 'Shamefully exorbitant', was John Delaval's comment. Indeed it was, looking at the bill everything is of the best, for instance *the use of the best Velvet Pall with gold Tossils, 20 days, £6, a set of the best ostridge feathers for hearse and horses, £10, (19a)*

Left to sort out Francis's debts, a long list of creditors looked to him for payment, but John would have none of it. The only person he paid anything to was Betty and he agreed to pay her the same allowance that Francis had paid her. John did nothing for Francis's children by Betty, but Fanny, his daughter, spent most of her time at the Mexboroughs. Young Francis, or Frank, took the name Delaval and as we shall see, made a life for himself.

Francis's death removed an ornament from society and a patriot, but was it a wasted life? A young friend, Richard Edgeworth, wrote that Francis: 'Invited me to his house, where probably, in six weeks I saw more of what is called the world than I should have seen in as many years'. (20) Cooke, the author of Foote's Memoirs wrote: 'Though indolent in his business he was active in his pleasures and so strongly did he possess the spirit of emulation that he would be the leading showman of his day whatever species of frivolity was the fashion. Yet with all these drawbacks on his character he was not deficient in either wit or learning'. (21) Foote on hearing that doctors wanted to examine his head at a post mortem said : 'I have known poor Frank these twenty-five years and I could never find any thing in it.' (22) Newspaper coverage of his death caused Walpole to note that: 'If I could have greater contempt for the age than I have it would be on observing that one single paragraph is all that has been said on our friend (the poet Thomas Gray) but when there are columns in every newspaper on Francis Delaval ought we not to be glad? Who would be a hero of their times?' (23) This of course was something of an exaggeration but there was coverage in most newspapers and much discussion on the cause of his death. Francis had made a will in 1770 leaving money to friends and family but he died heavily in debt so they received nothing. Popular tradition has associated him with fashionable amusement and gay revelry, but was he a selfish waster? Perhaps, but let us not forget that his death was lamented by rich and poor alike. He did earn a knighthood, he was elected as an MP, and he had mixed with royalty. He had lived life to the full.

A print of Delaval Hall showing structures which are not there now and probably were never built.

Notes on chapter nine

1.   *Horace Walpole's Correspondence, Vol. 20, p41*

2.   *The Gay Delavals, p38-45*

2A. *Survey of London 1931, vol 44, p142*

3.   *A Royal Affair, by Stella Tillyard, p62*

4.   *A.A. Vol 12 New Series, p225*

5.   *The Delaval Papers, p8*

6.   *ibid, p8*

7.   *The Monthly Chronicle 1887, p439*

8.   *County History Vol IX, p 164*

9.   *Memoirs of Richard Edgeworth by Himself, 1821, p117*

10. *Prince Edward Augustus was the younger brother of King George III. The Empress of Pleasure by Judith Summers 2003, p112*

11. *Horace Walpole's Correspondence, Vol. 9, p221*

11A. *The Trial of Francis Blake Delaval, 1755*

12. *The Gay Delavals, p120*

13. *The Delaval Papers, p9*

14. *A Royal Affair, p68*

15. *ibid, p69*

16. *The Gay Delavals, p107*

17. *A Royal Affair, p63*

18. *The Gay Delavals, p126*

19. *Memoirs of Richard Edgeworth, Vol I, p137*

19a *CRO Funeral expenses for Sir Francis Blake Delaval, 2DE /38/3/76 transcribed by Elspeth Gould*

20. *Memoirs of Richard Edgeworth, Vol I, p116*

21. *Memoirs of Samuel Foote by William Cooke. Men of Mark by Welford, p54*

22. *The Delaval Papers, p6*

23. *Walpole's correspondence, Vol. 28, p20*

CHAPTER TEN
JOHN AND THOMAS
MANAGER AND ENGINEER

John and Thomas were the second and fourth sons of Captain Francis and Rhoda. John was born in 1728, Thomas in 1731 and both were educated at Westminster School in London. They spent their holidays at Seaton, no doubt being led astray by brother Francis. He probably was the instigator of the fun and practical jokes but it was the skills of his brothers which made them happen. When John left school he went to Pembroke College, Cambridge but in typical Delaval fashion he was asked to leave after being accused of taking a young lady up to his room. Thomas Gray in a letter of 27th December 1746 described how John had boldly paraded: 'a certain gentle women properly call'd Nell Burnet - disguised as a Captain Hargraves in an officers habit throughout the town.' He then goes on to describe the Master of Pembroke Dr Long: 'felling and snuffleing about the bed in search of the young lady'. (1) He didn't find her, but John was asked to terminate his residency and leave. Fortunately he had just matriculated, but what his long-suffering father said is not recorded!

An old engraving of the 900 feet-long 'cut' through solid rock to create a new harbour at Seaton Sluice which opened in 1764.

Rhoda, the first child of Captain Francis Blake Delaval and Rhoda Apreece. An accomplished artist, she painted the faces of her brothers and sisters which were then sewn onto the canvas of this work completed by professional artist, Van Hawken.

Sir Francis Blake Delaval by Sir Joshua Reynolds. (Courtesy: Doddington Hall).

Sir John Delaval (1728-1808) by William Bell, 1774.

Sir John's wife, Susanna (1730-1783) by William Bell, 1770.

Miss Knight married Sir John Delaval, January 1803 at Earsdon to become the 2nd Lady Delaval. Miniature oval portrait by Samuel Shelley. (1795)

The Royal Northumberland Glassworks was producing over 1 million bottles a year by 1777. This photograph was taken before it was demolished in 1896.

After he finished his education, Thomas went abroad and spent some time in Hamburg as a merchant. He also took a keen interest in the latest industrial developments and it was there that he learnt about glass making.

Back at Seaton, John was helping his father manage the estates and falling in love with his cousin Susanna. She, you will recall, was the widow of Mr Potter and had come to Seaton with Betty Roach when her husband died. John and Susannah were married in April 1750 at the chapel in Dukes Street, Mayfair. Mr. Potter had left his wife a house in Albemarle Street, London, and this house was very convenient for John to stay when he attended Parliament.

For much of the time between 1754 and 1784 he was the M.P. for Berwick upon Tweed. He also spent a lot of time at his mother's estate at Doddington in Lincolnshire. Rhoda had inherited the beautiful brick built Tudor Manor house in 1749 on the death of her mother. John soon came to love Doddington and he devoted himself to renovating the somewhat neglected house and estate.

He planted trees to enrich the flat landscape and also planted a hop garden, the only one in Lincolnshire at the time.

The estates at Seaton continued to be worked in much the same way throughout the early part of the eighteenth century. There was mining and the export of coal, some salt manufacture and agriculture. In 1752, on the death of Captain Francis Blake Delaval, the income from the estate was worth about £9,000 per year. The Captain left everything to Francis with successive remainders to each of his other sons. It was not until 1755, when John took over the estates after coming to an agreement with Francis, that any sort of improvements could be noted. John had interests in Berwick, Seaton, London, Doddington and as we shall see later, at Ford. He was a gifted organiser and manager and his first step in running an enterprise was to appoint the best agent he could get to supervise on the spot. Then he would correspond on an almost daily basis with the agent. Wherever he was in the country he would write and receive letters. Many of the letters that agents sent to John have survived while most of the letters sent by John in reply have not. Instead of managing everything himself, where possible, he would lease out businesses to able people. For instance ship building in Seaton Sluice was leased out to Mr Topham in the 1760s.

Coal mining has always been difficult and dangerous. Deep mining was impossible until a method of pumping water out of mines was perfected. When John took over management of the estates about 6,500 chaldrons of coal (17,000 tons) were being exported annually from Seaton Sluice. (2) Nearly all of this coal went to London for domestic use. The air pollution caused by burning coal in this way is described by contemporary accounts as like a pall hanging over the capital and creating an eight month winter. Soot hung in the air and blocked out the sun. But of course the prosperity of North East England, particularly Newcastle, depended on this trade.

Only large coal was suitable for domestic fires but mining produced a lot of small coals which were of little use, so John, who had bought a half share in Hartley Collieries from Francis, set out to find a use for these small coals. To improve the efficiency of his coal mines John recruited William Brown of Throckley, one of the best mining engineers - or viewers as they were called then - in the area. In 1760 William made a mechanical pumping engine to take water out of the mine. In 1763, Joseph Oxley, another agent, designed a steam winding engine: ' for drawing coal out of the pit without employment of horses'. This machine was not a success so he redesigned it, and built a second one in 1765.This machine worked but was 'very apt to go wrong'. (3) Improvements were made and James Watt, the Scottish engineer, hearing of the new machine came to see it.

Frances and Sarah Hussey Delaval by William Bell, 1771.

John 'Jack' Delaval (1756-1775) the last male heir of the Delavals, by William Bell, 1773.

Sophia Anne, afterwards Mrs Jadis (1752-1793) by William Bell, 1770.

He made some improvements, one being the introduction of a fly wheel which made the machine run more smoothly. As the century progressed pumping engines designed by Thomas Newcomen were introduced which worked at low pressure. They were not very efficient and consumed large amounts of coal but they were able to pump water out of the mines, so deep mining became possible and thus coal production increased.

To get coal to the harbour at Seaton Sluice wagonways were used where horse drawn carts were pulled over wooden rails. An agreement in 1761 shows that John Young was to: 'Grease the Waggon Way and laid the Gutters from pits to the staves at 3s.6d. per week'. (4) It was at the harbour however that the real problem began. It simply wasn't big enough to handle the number of ships wanting to use the port. Coastal shipping was the only practical means of transport, so until the harbour was enlarged the industrial development planned for Seaton could not take place. William Brown told John in a letter written in April, 1761 to: 'Please to think of either mending your old harbour or making a New one'. (4)

John had been considering the problem for some time and in 1758 John Smeaton came to survey the harbour. He was famous for his work on the Eddystone lighthouse and he suggested building a long breakwater straight out from the beach north of the existing harbour to make a new dock. The plans showing this new dock are held by the Royal Society in London. John did not consider the plan suitable and no action was taken. John then consulted his brother Thomas and they resolved to make a cut eastwards through solid rock, from the existing harbour to the sea, so making a completely new entrance and dock.

Thomas supervised the work which started in September 1761 and was probably the biggest engineering project in the country at that time. The new cut, 900 feet long, 52 feet deep and 30 feet wide, took three years to complete. It would have been quicker to blast the rock away but the Delavals were much too thrifty. The sandstone rock was carefully quarried into measured lengths and sold. A pier was built out to protect the new entrance and great baulks of timber were collected to seal the entrance and keep the heavy seas out. The cut which cost about £10,000 was capable of handling 12 to 14 vessels of between 200 and 300 tons.

The harbour was opened on the 20th March 1764, when two ships under full sail entered the new dock. John provided a feast for the workmen and guests. Three roasted oxen and several sheep were eaten and plenty of strong ale was drunk to celebrate the opening. On the 22nd the Warkworth sailed out laden with 273 tons of coal. The new harbour soon proved its worth. Before the new harbour was built ships could only half load in port and had to finish loading in deeper water off shore. Ships could only make about seven round trips to London per year and the total tonnage exported never exceeded 6,500 chaldrons of coal. After 1764 ships could load a higher proportion of cargo before sailing and could make about ten round trips per year to London. By 1780 about 18,000 chaldrons of coal were exported annually. (5)

One other feature created by the new cut was that a new island was formed where the headland had been before. This became known as Rocky Island and a new bridge was made to link the island to the mainland. This bridge could be raised and lowered to allow tall sailing ships to pass through the cut. The wagon way had also to be re-routed to bring coals to the new dock.

However the cut did not solve all the problems of congestion and delay, many ships still couldn't load to full capacity unless they could set sail at high tide. Constant alterations were carried out to keep the harbour accessible. In 1772 the harbour was deepened and in 1797 the pier was rebuilt. Getting into the new cut was often difficult and many vessels came to grief trying to sail into the narrow entrance if the wind was against them. But the cut did enable Seaton Sluice to thrive. In 1777 records show that the port exported over 30,000 chaldrons of coal (double the usual yearly total), 300 tons of salt, 100 tons of copperas and over 1,000,000 bottles. (6)

The bottles were made in the glass works built by Thomas Delaval. Thomas had discovered the secrets of glass making when he was in Hamburg. John needed a use for the small unsaleable coal and glass proved the ideal solution. Work started on building The Royal Northumberland Glassworks around 1763. Initially all the materials were available locally - sea sand, small coals, clay for making moulds, kelp used as a flux, and salt. As production increased more raw materials were needed so the colliers came back to Seaton with sand, clay and ashes (burnt kelp) as ballast. Thomas brought some key workers over from Germany to teach the art of glass making to the local workmen. (7) By 1765 two glass cones and twenty-four men were producing 10,000 bottles a month. In 1766 Thomas took out a patent for black ware, of which he said, "we can make anything of it that is made in china or earthen ware." (8) The bottles made in the factory were exported to London in bottle sloops, ships similar to the collier brigs. John set up his own warehouse in London and Messrs Harrison and Broughton were his London agents overseeing the distribution of the bottles in the capital. In 1767, following the success of the bottle factory, Thomas started making window glass.

Another waste product of mining was iron pyrites or brasses. These lumps of mineral were non-combustible and had to be removed as there was no market for contaminated coal. To use these brasses, Thomas established beds for the extraction of copperas. The brasses were crushed and stored in heaps about three feet high. Water running over these heaps produced a mild acid which was distilled, using small coals, to make oil of vitriol or sulphuric acid. The residue iron oxide or copperas, was used in the glassworks as a pigment This primitive 'chemical industrial plant', proved quite successful and soon the supply of brasses from local mines ran out so brasses were imported for processing at the Copperas Factory from the Delaval's mine on the Ford estate. (9)

Salt had been manufactured and exported from the area since medieval times. Hartley Pans was the old name for Seaton Sluice, a name reflecting the salt-making industry. In the reign of Elizabeth I, there were up to eight salt pans producing about two tons of salt per week. This was a precarious business as six tons of coal were required to produce one ton of salt and the pans needed to be heated at white heat for three and a half days. Such harsh treatment meant that the salt pans rapidly deteriorated. (10) However, expensive as it was to produce, Hartley white salt was a sought-after commodity. It was used for curing fish and shipped to ports such as Hull and Yarmouth. By the later part of the eighteenth century production had risen to about 600 tons annually. Salt was being sold to the traditional fishing ports and also to Newcastle, Stockton and Yarm. In 1780 the government started to tax and regulate the salt trade. A tax was levied on salt imported into England from Scotland and this resulted in an increase in salt smuggling which damaged the industry. In 1785 regulations were brought in concerning the making of white salt and foul salt or alkali in the same pan. This made the trade more difficult and less profitable. In 1798 government regulations banned the making of white salt and alkali together. This effectively killed the manufacture of white salt. Some salt making continued so as to supply the alkali to the glass works, where it was used as a flux, but the salt trade ceased. By 1820 salt panning had died out completely. It was the industrial mining of salt, in places like Cheshire, that finally killed off salt production from salt water.

The prosperity of the Delaval enterprises depended on coastal shipping to transport their products. Yet, surprisingly they didn't own any ships and left the responsibility of transporting goods to others. Sea transport was a risky business, many ships were lost and it appears this was a risk the Delavals were not prepared to take. Lists of ships using the harbour show that many were locally owned. As shipping increased so did the risk of damage. Shipwrights at

Seaton Sluice could deal with minor repairs but major repairs were carried out on the Tyne at Shields. John decided to profit from the increasing need for ships by opening a shipyard at Seaton Sluice. Not wishing to run the yard himself, he found a master boat-builder, a Mr Topham, who leased the yard. In 1767 one of the first ships to be built, the George and Thomas, a ship of about 75 tons, was sold to a Mr William Dobson for £263 2s 6d. Ship building flourished and ships were being built at Seaton Sluice at least until 1796.

All this industrial activity required new buildings so in 1766 a brick yard was opened. The local sandstone was quarried and used for building and paving and occasionally some was exported. The many thirsty workmen demanded beer so a brewery was built and public houses followed. It was said that on the quayside there were seven pubs, one for each day of the week. The workmen employed in all these enterprises needed housing. Between 1771 and 1781, almost fifty houses were built in the Glasshouse estate. The cost of a typical workman's house was £35 8s. Thirty-one new houses were built at Hartley for £570 and new houses at Seaton village cost £114 12s 9d. Shops were needed and at least four were built including premises for a barber, a grocer and a blacksmith.

To help feed the workers, a slaughterhouse was built and a new windmill was erected at Bleakley Hill. To look after the welfare of the community, John provided a village school and and a doctor. (11) It was the Delavals' belief that everything the workers needed should be available in the village.

In 1761 the newly crowned George III, perhaps in recognition of his abilities and public spirit, created John a baronet, and from then on he was known as Sir John Hussey Delaval (Hussey was his wife's family name). Although John spent a lot of time running his businesses he still found time for politics. As he owned the large estate at Ford he decided to stand as MP for Berwick upon Tweed. Somewhat to everyone's surprise his opponent in 1754 was the London journalist, John Wilkes, who later achieved notoriety when his attacks on the government of Lord Bute in 1763 led to him being arrested and sent to the Tower for seditious libel.

In 1770 Wilkes successfully campaigned for the right to publish verbatim reports of Parliament and he gained the title of 'The Father of English Liberty'. Wilkes rather naively told the Berwick electorate that: 'as I will never take a bribe, so I will never offer one.' (12) Needless to say he wasn't elected. Afterwards Wilkes petitioned the House of Commons, accusing Delaval of bribery. A half empty House was preparing itself for a dreary round of charge and counter-charge when it was suddenly enlivened by a speech from Delaval

The Accommodating Spouse: (*TYR . .NN . .Es delight! Coming York over her: or what you like).
James Aitkin, 1789. (National Portrait Gallery). (See page 102).

The hatchment of Sir John Hussey Delaval (1728-1808) is displayed in the Church of Our Lady.
The Delaval coat of arms are shown in the first and fourth quartering.

The Earl and Countess of Mexborough, nee Sarah Delaval (1742-1821) attending the coronation of George 111, by Sir Joshua Reynolds. (Courtesy: Doddington Hall).

'full of whit, humour, and buffoonery.' (13) Listening in the gallery, with growing indignation to the uproar, was the Chief Minister Pitt (the Elder). As soon as Delaval sat down he strode into the chamber. His first words silenced the House, and to the consternation of members he sided with Wilkes!

In Parliament, John tended to support the government but as the voters of Berwick thought he had neglected them he did not stand in 1761. But his successor as MP for Berwick died, so in 1765, supported by the government and the Duke of Northumberland, John again stood for election. He was returned as MP after, according to some sources, brazenly bribing the electors. The election was said to have cost him over £6,000. From then on he retained the confidence of the electorate and was returned at each election until 1774. In trying to improve his position in the county John had carefully cultivated the friendship of the Duke of Northumberland and, when he had taken over the estates from Francis, he wrote a rather pompous letter to the Duke informing him he now owned all the estate. In 1774, when the Duke suggested he stood with his son for the Northumberland seat, he deserted Berwick. However the electors did not like the Duke's tactics and John was not elected. In 1780 his old constituents at Berwick accepted him back without a contest.

To ensure his business and political interests ran smoothly, John travelled widely. He kept in touch by writing letters many of which have survived. He wrote to his wife in affectionate terms, "I arrived my angel here yesterday... and am as happy to have come as I can be without my dear girl.. I am yours forever." Susanna replied to her husband's letters but unfortunately none of these have survived. They appear to have had a happy marriage as they had six children. Their only son John was born in 1756 and her last daughter Sarah was born in 1763. John and Susanna had a rich social life, at least in their early years. In the archives are cards inviting Mr and Mrs Delaval to visit friends for dinner, to play cards, etc; with the great and the good.

When John was at Seaton, he would join in family revels, particularly if they were acting a play, but it should be remembered that Seaton was officially Francis's residence until he handed it over to John just before he died. John recorded his growing family by commissioning local artist William Bell to paint full length portraits of himself and Lady Delaval, young John and his daughters Sophia, Sarah, Frances and Elizabeth. John obviously took a liking to William Bell as he employed him to teach drawing to his children and he eventually paid him a pension of fifty pounds a year and provided him with a cottage. (14)

John did not spend much time at Delaval Hall. He was very fond of Doddington and spent much of his time there. He was responsible for redecorating the interior in the simple and elegant style of the 1760s which is unchanged to this day. He brought many of the best paintings to the house, including fine family portraits which are still on display. Among the paintings are two by Sir Joshua Reynolds, one shows John's sister Sarah and her husband, The Earl of Mexborough, at the coronation of George III. The other picture shows Sir Francis in his army uniform. When John wanted to send large items such as beds or pianos from Seaton to Doddington they were loaded onto colliers and sent by sea. In the state bedrooms, John had 16th century Flemish tapestries nailed to the walls. He also added the elegant staircase, enlarged the windows and installed double glazing but he left the oak panelling installed by the Hussey Family in the parlour. (15)

When Francis died, John had a problem, he now officially owned both Doddington and Seaton which was forbidden under the terms of Rhoda's will, and Edward wanted to live at Doddington. A long, acrimonious legal battle followed and, at one point when John thought he would lose his beloved Doddington, he ordered all the trees on the estate to be felled. Eventually however a compromise was reached and John agreed to buy out his brother and he continued to live at Doddington. The woodland was only replaced when Edward gained control after John's death.

As we have noted it was Thomas Delaval who had supervised the construction of the new harbour and glass works which eventually covered four and a half acres of land. Initially two huge cones were built and a third was added in 1788. There were four ovens in each cone, and a team of four men worked each oven: a gatherer who collected the molten glass, a blower who made the bottle, an apprentice, and the most skilled man, a finisher, who sealed the bottle.

The finished bottles were loaded into carts which ran on rails down through a network of tunnels to the quayside. (16) At the quay they were loaded into baskets, hoisted on to the bottle sloops and packed into holds by loaders. The workmen were refreshed by draughts of ale brought to them by women employed as ale carriers. The bottles were shipped mainly to London where they sold for between 20d and 30d per dozen. Breakages were about one bottle in thirty. The bottles varied in size from 5 gallons down to half a pint.

The Delaval enterprises were doing well but there was disagreement among the brothers. Francis being the eldest, officially owned the estates but was prepared to let the others manage them in return for a yearly income. But of course as we have seen, Francis was always in debt and trying to get more income from the estate. As a result of one of these arguments, Thomas took over the management of the colliery as well as the glass works. Thomas generously increased Francis's allowance by £500 per year and acted as guarantor for a loan to Francis of £10,000 by his sister Sarah Mexborough.

Thomas was an engineer and not really a manager, and after a while he found he was unable to pay the interest on the estate mortgages and meet the liabilities involved in running the colliery and the glassworks. He was forced to go to John at Doddington and negotiate a way out of his difficulties. John agreed to buy out Thomas completely releasing him from all his obligations at Seaton in return for an income of £1,000 per year. At the same time he sorted out Francis's affairs, and so John gained complete control over all the estates.

The one outstanding problem was who was going to pay Francis's creditors? Thomas insisted he be released from acting as guarantor for the £10,000 owing to the Mexboroughs. John refused to pay and eventually it was agreed it should be a charge on the estate payable when young John was twenty-one. In fact the debt was never repaid and the Mexboroughs had to sell their property at Cannons. John drove a hard bargain. Thomas, who had contributed a great deal to the success of the industries at Seaton, was not generously rewarded.

In 1768 Thomas had married Cecilia Watson, a wealthy lady from Clapham in London.They had one child Louisa, who died young and was buried in The Church of Our Lady. After being paid off by John in 1772, Thomas retired to London. He tried on several occasions to get into parliament but was never elected. Thomas died a typical Delaval death. He was, according to the Gentleman's Magazine: 'taking an airing on horse back in Hyde Park when he dropped from his horse in a fit.' (17) He died in August 1787, aged fifty six years old.

Meanwhile, John was continuing to support the coalition government, headed by Charles James Fox and Lord North. In 1783 he ' rose as a country gentleman just to say he had a high regard for his majesty's ministers.' Later that year his support was rewarded with an Irish peerage. King George was against the coalition and refused to appoint any more English Peers because they would have seats in the House of Lords. Generally, Irish peers were not so privileged, only a small number of representative peers were given seats in the Lords. So John continued as MP for Berwick. As his political career flourished sadly his wife's health deteriorated. Susanna put on weight and at one point weighed over 15 stone. She withdrew from society. Other members of the family played hostess at Delaval Hall. Tired and worn out Susanna died in October 1783, aged 53. She was buried in Westminster Abbey with the full honours due to a peeress of the realm. On the floor of St Paul's Chapel in the abbey is a stone slab with an inscription which reads "Here lieth the body of the Right

Honourable Susanna Baroness Delaval who departed this life October 1st 1783". The inscription also goes on to record the internment of Sir John and his daughter Sarah who are both buried there.

In 1786 John voted against the coalition on the controversial India Bill and supported the young Prime Minister William Pitt by voting for his parliamentary reform proposals. He was rewarded by Pitt with an English peerage and a seat in the House of Lords. He became John Hussey Baron Delaval on the 21st August 1786 and took his seat in the House of Lords on 23rd January 1787. His volte face is recorded in the satirical poem The Rollaid. (18)

From 1772 John had complete control over the estates at Seaton, Doddington, Ford and Dissington. The Dissington estate had been inherited from his father. Most of it was sold by 1763 although some agricultural land at South Dissington remained in the family until the 1800s. The Doddington Estate consisted of about 2,430 acres of agricultural land bringing in a rental income of around £1,300 per year. John appointed as estate steward, William Portes, who was originally employed as a joiner at Seaton Delaval Hall.

Portes worked for many years at Doddington and was eventually pensioned off when Edward took over Doddington. (19)

At Seaton, John had a small group of trusted agents to help him manage his various enterprises. His superintendent and auditor was a Mr Watson. He retired in 1780 and John Bryers took his place. George Douglas was the General Inspector. William Brown was a Viewer and looked after the coal mines. When he resigned to run his own mines a Mr Allen was appointed. Joseph Oxley spent much of his time supervising the Ford estate and Mr Manchester was the glassworks manager. Mr Cowper was the overseer of salt pans and labourers, and there was also a book keeper, a warehouse keeper and a general storehouse keeper. Despite temporary fluctuations trade flourished at Seaton. An idea of the wealth created can be gained from the following figures. Duty paid to the crown in 1779 came to almost £25,000. (20) Equivalent to nearly £2,000,000 in today's money.

This was made up as follows-

	£	S	D
Coal 23,000 Chaldrons.	16100	0	0
Salt 500 tons. Duty £5 14s 1d per ton	2852	1	8
Copperas 70 tons, Duty	15	0	0
Glass Duty paid July 1777-July 1778	4415	11	6
Brewery ale	510	9	9
Brewery malt duty paid	184	2	10
Other Duties paid	300	0	0
TOTAL	**24377**	**5**	**9**

Production was increased at the bottle works. New round cones replaced the original square cones and these proved more efficient and less prone to catch fire. In 1777-1778, 145,618 dozen bottles were made. Of these, 120,524 went to Harrison in London. Attempts were made to find new markets but they had only limited success. In 1775 the work force was about 63 and by 1778 it had risen to 96. By 1796 over 200,000 dozen bottles a year were being made, the vast majority going to Harrison and Broughton in London and this level of production continued until about 1806. (21). Glassmaking continued for much of the 19th century but on a much reduced scale. The last shipment of bottles was exported in 1872 bound for the Channel Islands. In December 1896 demolition work began on the huge brick cones. Today the site is occupied by residential accommodation.

Coal was the commodity on which everything else depended. In 1774 there were five working pits in the Hartley area. Then, the life of a pit was rarely more than five years, because once the workings reached a certain level, they become difficult to ventilate, were liable to flood and underground transport became too expensive. Over the next 25 years a further 24 pits were sunk. (22) As pits closed and others opened, the wagonway needed to be extended. In 1784, with the Chathem pit about to be sunk, it became necessary to carry a branch of the wagonway across the Seaton Burn. A letter from John Crooks at Hartley Colliery to Sir John suggests that a bridge be constructed: 'in the Hungry Banks at or about the middle distance between the old engine quarry and the plantations'. (23) The Hungry Banks refers to the village allotment site. In 1785 a timber bridge was built at the point suggested. It had 23 supporting legs, at its highest was over 40 feet tall and cost £344 to build. It was a very impressive structure and it stood for about one hundred years carrying the wagonway across the burn. To extend the wagonway across the bridge 1,144 yards of new rail was laid. From the account books we can see that wooden rails were still used, beech rails cost 5d per yard and oak rails cost 7d. The cost of laying the track was 4 shillings per yard. A branch of the wagonway went to the bottle works and a branch went to the three coal shoots on the south side of the quay. In 1797 this branch was extended to the Nightingale pit near the Dairy House and subsequently became part of the Blyth and Tyne railway. (24)

In addition to the industrial side we should not forget that farming and the rearing of game for hunting and shooting formed an important part of the estate. There are many letters in the archives from agents and gamekeepers to Sir John about estate management. A typical letter from 1788 asks for: 'one of the gardener's assistants to fed the dogs, walk with them out two or three days every week and take care of the ferrets, which will allow him greater liberty to look after poachers....but for him ....to see and examine the traps in hare park, pheasant ground etc., and the heads and skins of all vermin to be nailed upon the Coach House doors.' Pheasant rearing was an important activity another letter from April 1783 mentions that: 'Richard Whorley has 200 pheasants eggs which are very promising for hatching well.' (25) Foxes were a constant threat to the game birds and so hunting with dogs became a regular feature of country life. Pheasants and other game were an important part of the diet of the gentry and of course they were a great temptation to the hungry, poorer classes. Poaching was a constant threat and gamekeepers spent a lot of time and effort protecting the game.

Besides Doddington and Seaton, John also had the Ford Estate to manage. When he took over the estate in 1756, it consisted of about 7,000 acres of poor, open scrubland, much of it wet and boggy without hedges or fences. Some of this land was worth as little as 2s per acre. The castle was also in a poor state of repair. John appointed Joseph Oxley to be steward at the Ford Estate. He was an excellent choice, an able administrator with a scientific frame of mind.

A married man with six children, he moved up to Ford in 1765 and was paid £60 per year and given a cottage, free coals and a cow.

John realised that the first thing needed to make the estate profitable was to improve the quality of the land. So work started on clearing the scrubland. Drainage schemes were started and hedges planted to enclose the land. A tree nursery was started to grow the hedge plants, and lime kilns were built to produce lime to spread on the poor acid soils. Grass was planted on the improved soil and as the land was enclosed it was let off to tenants The rental income for the estate in 1760 was £1086.11s. In 1793 Oxley sent a return to the

Board of Agriculture and from this document we can see how the land was improved. Over this thirty year period, 92 miles of quickset hedges and stone walls were raised on the estate.

To do this 488,000 'quicks'(hedge plants) were grown plus 15,000 trees. Four men were constantly employed on this task and the cost over thirty years was £4,076.Thirteen new farm houses were built and old ones improved at a cost of £5,000. John insisted that the farms were let out to men who knew the land. He disliked 'gentlemen farmers.' In 1794 income from farm rents came to £4,868.14s.4d. (26)

Farmers need metal tools to work with and in 1769 a Forge Mill was established. Iron was imported from Sweden and agricultural tools were soon being sold in Wooler and Kelso. The forge was leased out for £30 per year. To meet the estate's demand for building materials a brick works was started. Managed by a Mr. Turner, it produced 120,000 bricks and 74,000 pantiles a year. In 1788 Oxley's son, Ben, took over the lease.

There was also a colliery on the Ford Estate at Ford Moss which was never very productive. It suffered from flooding and in spite of pumping machinery being introduced the first tenant went bankrupt.

There were three corn mills on the estate including one opposite the forge on the River Till at Heatherslaw where there had been a water mill for hundreds of years. This was reconstructed at a cost of £750 around 1760. For a time Oxley acted as the miller but in 1767 he became acquainted with: ' a baker from South Shields who readily joined with me in partnership as I had not the capital to carry on myself'. Another letter from Oxley to John shows how enterprising he was: 'July 1767 Sir with this I send the accounts. As the wool is now in hand I have set apart about 10 stone for the experiment in the Blanket Factory. I have already done something toward fitting up the long barn at Heatherslaw ….. for the weaving shop. Nothing can be done towards the Fulling mill until my Lady Delaval comes down.The smith shop is now at work'. (27) In 1769 John Darling took over the mill and also married Oxley's daughter Margaret. She took over the lease of the mill when he died in 1782.

John also had Ford Castle to look after. Starting in 1760, he spent about £10,500 on the dilapidated medieval castle turning it into a Gothic building to make it 'a useful and noble country seat.' (28) John knew how to look after his tenants and he knew how to party as the following extract shows. 'Upwards of five hundred tenants and servants assembled at Ford Castle where they were entertained with the utmost liberty. Fifty of the most seasonable dishes were placed on each table, a large fat ox was prepared; and the liquor, which was plentifully supplied, was of the very best quality. One hundred and fifty gallons of rum, eighty gallons of brandy. One hundred and eighty bottles of wine, one bowl of punch contained eighteen gallons of spirit, six stones of sugar and forty lemons.' Some party! Mackenzie writing shortly after John's death said: 'The memory of Sir John Delaval is highly honoured in Northumberland. He employed his ample wealth in cultivating and improving his estates and in dispensing felicity to innumerable families. The country round Ford, he divided and enclosed with excellent hedges and clothed the bare hills with fine plantations.' (29).

Running a large business is never easy and in the Delaval letters there are many examples of problems and many were to do with disagreement and jealousy between the various agents. Oxley seemed to attract a lot of jealous criticism partly because of the way he helped his children to get on. One letter says: 'My Lord This comes with my Duety to you and to informe your Lordship of the afears at Ford. I have ben ther this 5 weeks and I have seed a great Deall of Rogrey which I canot hied from you nor do I think it proper I should.' (30) The letter goes on to accuse Oxley of letting a contract to his son for less than another would pay. John however had confidence in Oxley and let him carry on. But John's problems were not confined to business. Most of his children died before him and the rest of the family were always trying to get money from him.

About a year after his wife's death, Sir John embarked on a curious relationship with a young girl, Miss Elizabeth Hicks, who was in her early teens. At first he seemed to treat her like a granddaughter when he took her around the country. Oddly she didn't stay in the family house with Sir John but in a little house especially provided for her. At Seaton and Ford Castle she stayed in little estate cottages. (31) The first mention of her at Seaton is in September 1785 when her name and weight were recorded in the visitors book. She weighed 10 stone 12 lbs. When Sir John was at Doddington she stayed in the rectory which was empty since the death of the incumbent. In London she stayed in a small house at Milburn Place, just around the corner from the Delaval townhouse in Hanover Square. At Claremont, the estate he bought for Sarah and her husband, the Earl of Tyrconnel, he had a cottage built especially for her. What Sir John saw in her is not known, she was a typical rebellious teenager. In 1786 a letter was written to Sir John requesting his Lordship to quit his London ladgings because of the repeated misbehaviour of Miss Hicks and her boot boy. The letter goes on "there is a continual...scene of noise and riot... such behaviour is practiced in his lordship's absence." The writer concludes that the servants are too much their own master and mistress when John is away. No action appears to have been taken. Presumably Sir John smoothed things over.

In 1788 Elizabeth's horse is listed in the stables at Delaval Hall when she was about 15 years old. An entry in the visitors book shows her weight increased to 12 stone. She was now living the good life and she had become John's mistress. That they shared a bed is made clear in a letter sent to the servants at Delaval Hall instructing them to warm their bed before the fire and have it slept in every night while they were away. (32)

Another indication of their relationship is the way she spent money on clothes and finery. Between August 1792 and August 1793 she spent £223 on clothes which included about £50 on hats and £17 on shoes. Elizabeth had a weakness for Moroccan slippers. In the four months from January to April 1793 she bought a dozen pairs of slippers at 8s 6d (42 1/2p) a pair. Compare that with the wages of a typical maid who would earn about £10 a year. The dressmakers' bill unfortunately doesn't tell us how many garments were made but we have a bill from 1794 showing two receipts, one for £5.1shilling and one for £9.4 shillings, from Albrightof London for gowns for Miss Hicks. In 1778 there is a bill for £15.14 shillings for jewellery from John Deards Goldsmiths, London. The bill is for Sir John but it's a fair bet that the jewellery was for Elizabeth. Similarly the bills to Sir John for two silk umbrellas suggest he was indulging her. Elizabeth spent a fair amount of time in London. In July and August 1795 she was at Milburn Place. During that time a butcher's bill shows that about 20 head of poultry, including ducks, geese and chickens, were delivered there at a cost of £2.15 shillings. A list of servants employed by Sir John in 1795 shows just two servants for Milburn Place, a gardener and a maid. Presumably they would look after the property when Elizabeth was away. When she stayed there other servants would come from the London properties. Sir John was fond of Elizabeth but she wasn't really a suitable companion for a baronet, she was poorly educated and probably illiterate. To help Elizabeth feel at ease in society, a Mrs Walshingham was employed at a guinea a week to teach her the art of being a lady, this included dancing, music and French!

Miss Hicks didn't have all of Sir John's attention. In the Delaval's weight book, the entry on August 8th, 1786, records the weight of Miss Charlotte Knight as 9 stone 2lbs. Charlotte was probably employed as a servant but she soon became a companion, then mistress and eventually wife of Sir John. Charlotte was a much more suitable partner than Elizabeth. Records show that she was baptised Susanna Knight at St Benet's Church in London in November 1762. (Curiously she was known as Charlotte by some members of the family.) Charlotte, or Susanna as I will call her from now on, was ten years older than Elizabeth and, a proper lady, she was also literate.

How this menage-a-trois worked in practice is not recorded but perhaps one reason Miss Hicks had her own cottages at the Delaval houses is so that she could stay there while Miss Knight held court in the main house. That Miss Knight took a position nearer to a wife is apparent in the correspondence to her, that she had influence over Sir John is not in doubt, for her brother Henry and his family came to live on the Delaval estate.

Late in 1795 Miss Hicks returned to Seaton Delaval suffering from what was said to be consumption. The cold winter did nothing for her and she died at the age of only 23 years in February 1796. Sir John placed a touching obituary in the Newcastle Chronicle. "Died Thursday last at Seaton Delaval Miss Elizabeth Hicks whose admirable goodness of heart and sweetness of manners, rendered her most dear to all who had the pleasure of being acquainted with her."

Elizabeth was buried in the vault at the Church of Our Lady. Her death solved a problem for Sir John. Now he had only one young lady to live with. We have no idea what Miss Hicks looked like, no pictures of her have been identified. We are much more fortunate with Miss Knight, we have a superb miniature portrait of her by Samuel Shelley painted about 1795. This 7cm oval shows an attractive young lady who would be a suitable companion for Sir John. Susanna was also spending Sir John's money and also bought Moroccan slippers but not in the same quantities as Elizabeth Hicks. In four months in 1793 Elizabeth spent £6.4 shillings on slippers while Susanna spent £4.7 shillings in a similar period. Comparing bills for clothes it appears that Susanna spent a lot less than Elizabeth. However Susanna was fond of new gloves. In 1799 there is a receipt for £10.16 shillings for gloves from William Bilton of Newcastle. There are also bills for half a hundred hair pins and lavender water. That Miss Knight was taking on the role of Sir John's wife is evident from the menu for dinner in December 1797. After the food comes a list of those dining. A typical list might include Lord Strathmore, Lord Tyrconnel, Mrs Knight, Count Catnallen, Mr G. Tucket.

In 1800 Sir John's favourite daughter, Sarah, died. The only people left close to him were Sarah's daughter, his granddaughter, Susan Carpenter, his daughter Francis and Miss Knight. The Knight family were increasingly helped by Sir John. In 1803 Susanna's brother Henry and family moved into Seaton Cottage and there are letters from "E.Young, your affectionate and loving aunt", thanking "you and his lordship for the payment of your annual bounty."

In January 1803, in a simple ceremony at Earsdon Parish Church, Susana Knight and Sir John Delaval were married. The wedding was a small family affair. The witnesses were local people and not the nobility.

The question often asked is why did they get married after living together so long. One suggestion is that it would legitimise any children but as Susanna was over forty I don't think this was a consideration. I think John was genuinely fond of her and wanted her to be secure when he died. The widow of a peer would be in a much stronger position than an ex-mistress.

During the later years of the 18th century the peace and prosperity of Britain was badly shaken by the almost continuous war with France. The Delavals, like other rich families, saw their standard of living fall. The days of lavish excess were over. The threat of invasion was taken very seriously.

In August 1795, The Duke of York brought thirteen regiments of horse and foot, 7,000 men altogether, to exercise on Blyth beach, and most of the local population came to watch. Sir John entertained The Duke of Gloucester and senior officers at Delaval Hall, but he was worried that the common soldiers would trespass on his estate and poach his game. John ordered extra security measures to be put in force.

He had more walls and fences built and made sure that the porter's lodges were manned. He also offered a five pound reward to anyone identifying a poacher. One other consequence of having a large number of idle soldiers around was that over the next few months pregnant girls from Seaton Sluice were busy arranging hasty marriages to reluctant soldiers.

The real danger however came from the sea, from French privateers. They cruised the seas around Britain looking for ships to capture. Several collier brigs were taken and crews and ships were held to ransom. In March 1801, The Honoured left Seaton Sluice about 8 o'clock and was captured off St. Mary's Island at 10 o'clock by a French lugger privateer. (33)

Unfortunately the Royal Navy could not get enough sailors to volunteer to man its ships and so was unable to protect coastal shipping. It resorted to using the press gang and this resulted in many merchant ships being undermanned. A letter from John's agent, Stephen Watson, mentions: 'Difficulty in getting sailors as all pressed in to the navy-the present hot press for sailors has stopped all trade.' (34) To counter the threat of invasion, John helped to organise a local defence force, The Seaton Delaval Volunteers. Captain John Bryers, Sir John's agent, was one of the officers. Preparations were made to defend the coast and evacuate civilians.

Such was the atmosphere at the time, it was reported in one newspaper that a French ship had landed its crew and sacked Delaval Hall. This of course was not true. (35)

There was one further enterprise that John was involved with that has not been mentioned so far and that was banking. It was a risky business, bank failures were frequent and sometimes a run on a bank was caused by nothing more than a rumour. Sir John banked with the Newcastle bank of Surtees and Burdon. In 1793 there was a crisis in the banking system caused by the outbreak of war with France. Depositors tried to withdraw their money but the banks could not pay everyone. In Newcastle the banks were besieged by creditors and forced to close for a while then resumed business when things calmed down.

A committee of local businessmen, of which Sir John was a member, was set up to support the banks. In 1797 and 1803 the Surtees and Burdon Bank was again in difficulty, and by 1806 the bank was insolvent and its partners declared bankrupt. In 1811, a sale of assets was held at the Turk's Head, Newcastle, but the affair dragged on until 1832 when a final dividend of only 8d in the pound was paid. (36) A hand-written document from 1806 shows Sir John's rage and frustration. Violent crossing out would indicate that he had a substantial amount invested in the bank. The note appears to show that the bank owed £348,000 and had assets of only £2,000. (37)

How much money Sir John lost is not clear but it must have been a substantial amount. He appears to have lost his savings but the estate rents and income from various enterprises kept the estate from bankruptcy.

John died peacefully in May 1808 and was buried beside his first wife in Westminster Abbey. Dying without a male heir, his titles expired with him. Under the terms of his father's will, the entailed estates of Seaton and Doddington passed to his brother Edward. The remainder of the estate he left to his wife. This included Ford Castle and the Bottle works. Thus Seaton and Ford were separated, so the curse of the Dalavals was broken. The Delavals could die peacefully in their beds again. (38)

John was the rock at the centre of the family. They looked to him for help, advice and, most of all, money. He ran the estates and generated the income and so controlled the purse strings. John had the vision to see what was possible and the drive to make it happen. He changed the Ford Estate from overgrown scrubland to best farming practice. He turned Seaton Sluice from a small port into an industrial centre. He decorated the interior of Doddington Hall so well that it has never been altered. He undertook civic duties and for many years was an MP. He was a patron of the arts and like all Delavals loved the theatre. His death was a great loss to many charitable and philanthropic institutions in the county.

He was a proud Northumbrian and always supported his native county. His personal life was tinged with sadness as his first wife, most of his brothers and sisters, and his own children, all died before him. But he retained the loyalty of his workforce and the respect of all who knew him. However sad and lonely he may have been, he did not give up. To keep up appearances, he ordered that the Hall be repainted and his last public duty was the enrolment of volunteers in the local defence force.

Sir John's notes showing that Surtees and Burdon Bank was insolvent in 1806. NB –Carr was John's agent. Brummel was a Morpeth solicitor who was well-known in banking circles.

The parterre garden at Seaton Delaval Hall.

Notes on chapter ten

1. *Thomas Gray, A Life, by L. Mach, p358. Also Correspondence of Thomas Gray, V1 by Toynbee 1935*

2. *Unpublished thesis in Blyth Library. The Industrial Development of Seaton Sluice by R. A. Foster, p32. A chaldron was a volumetric unit of measure used in the coal trade. Its absolute value varied in time and place. Its imperial equivalent in 1616 was 43 cwt and 53 cwt after 1695. A London chaldron was different to a Newcastle chaldron. See Ports and Harbours of Northumberland, Stafford Linsley, p210*

3. *Delaval Papers, p166*

4. *Letter County Record Office, 2DE 6/3/13, 1761*

5. *Foster, p32*

6. *Linsley, p183*

7. *Among the papers at Ford we found the original agreement between Thomas Delaval and the burgmaster of Nieburg in Hanover for obtaining men from 'thence to teach the art of making glass' in the new glass works at Hartley. Society in the Last Century, 1878*

8. *Foster, p24. Bottle sloops were shallow drafted in order to lie under the bottle crane at Seaton Sluice and had a striking mast in order to pass under London Bridge. Four locally-owned sloops carried between 3,000 and 4,500 dozen bottles per trip.*

9. *Foster p21*

10. *From Border to Middle Shire, p53*

11. *The first doctor was Dr Paxton who practised from about 1760 to 1800. He was followed by his grandson, George Ochiltree*

12. *The Gay Delavals, Francis Askham, p77*

13. *The Life of William Pitt, early of Chatham, p255*

14. *Eighteenth Century Newcastle, P.M. Horsley, p156*

15. *Doddington Hall and Gardens Guide Book, J and C Birch*

16. *Foster p25*

17. *The Gentleman's Magazine 1787, p839*

18. *The House of Lords in The Age of Reform, A.S.Turberville. Peerage, p445.*
    The Rolliad, a contemporary satirical poem, p63.
    It comments thus.
    "The nobel convert , Berwick's honoured choice,
    That faithful echo of the people's voice,
    One day ,to gain an Irish title glad,
    For Fox he voted-so the people bade;
    'Mongst English Lords ambitious grown to sit,
    Next day the people bade him vote for Pitt
    To join the stream, our patriot, nothing loth,
    By turns discreetly gave his voice to both"

19. *History of the Manor and township of Doddington, R.E.G. Cole 1897*

20. *Foster p7*

21. *Foster p25. Ultimately there were six glass cones in operation, named Hartley, Waterford, Galligan, Bias, Charlotte and Success.*

22. *Proceedings of the Society of Antiquaries, Third series Vol. VII 1916 p73*

23. *Procedings of the Society of Antiquaries, p77*

24. *ibid*

25. *Delaval Papers, p75-77*

26. *The Ford Estate in the 1750s and Thereafter, Joseph Oxley, answers to questions from the Board of Agriculture 1793*

27. *Letter in County Record Office 2DE 4/10/24, 1776*

28. *Ford at the Time of the Waterfords, 1822-1907, J. Joicey, p3*

29. *View of Northumberland, E. Mackenzie 1825, p69*

30. *Letter in County Record Office 2DE 4/61/8, 1788*

31. *Mackenzie 1825 Vol. 11, p424*

32. *Delaval Papers, p79*

33. *Press Gangs and Privateers,1993, p63*

34. *Letter County Record Office, 2DE/4/3/28, 1779*

35. *Delaval Papers p151*

36. *History of Banks and Banking in Northumberland, Maberly Phillips 1894, p53*

37. *County Records Office, 2DE/35/15/1*

38. *The Will of Sir John Delaval is stored at the Berwick Record Office NRO 2802/12*

CHAPTER ELEVEN
SONS AND DAUGHTERS

In this chapter we will look at the lives of the other children of Captain Francis and Rhoda. About some of them we know very little beyond their names and birth dates. Others, as we shall see, have a story to tell.

Their daughter Anne, born in December 1737, was said to be an amiable little girl with a mischievous face and she was known as 'Little Monk'. Brought up at Delaval Hall, her education was good for a girl of the time. She was taught to read and write, to speak French and Italian and she inherited the Delaval love of theatre, taking part in productions and often playing the part of Calista in The Fair Penitent. In the summer of 1759, after the death of her mother, she went to Brighton. She hated the London life and much preferred the clean air and peace of the seaside. Here, she met Sir William Stanhope. The story of their relationship is told in a series of letters. The first written by his brother, the Earl of Chesterfield, to Arthur Stanhope on the 28th September says: 'I must now inform you of an event with which you will have no great reason to be pleased, and at which I confess that I was very much surprised. About ten days ago my brother communicated to me his resolution to marry Miss Delaval- and as for the lady she has been soberly and modestly educated in the country, and is of a very good gentleman's family. She is young enough to have children, being but two and twenty, and brother is not too old to beget some, so that probably there will be children'. (1) Sir William was sixty-two, had been married twice before and was going deaf.

Miss Stanhope wrote to her brother in October: 'I found Sir William who at once told me that he was to be married - to Miss Delaval, a young lady of twenty two, whom he saw for the first time at Brighthelmstone, three weeks ago. It surprised me a little, though I have told you I thought such a thing very likely.' That the family were worried about the outcome of this marriage is evident from the letters. In October, Arthur Stanhope wrote: 'The event of Sir William's marriage is undoubtedly a great disappointment to us.'

Two years after their marriage, Sir William and Anne set out for Florence where they hoped the warmer winter climate would help Anne recover from a recent miscarriage. There is a note in the correspondence of the poet Thomas Gray concerning the couple on their continental tour, a Mr Cradock writes: 'No expense was spared that her (Anne's) natural genius might be improved during her travels on the continent. She spoke French and Italian correctly, and had great taste for both painting and sculpture.

As we were retiring from the old Louvre, one of the Academicians said' Have you many more such ladies in England? She is indeed a prodigy' (2) Alas, however the marriage did not survive the tour. Their return is described in a letter from Walpole to Sir Horace Mann. As their carriage returned to Blackheath, Sir William got out, made her a low bow, and said: 'Madam I hope I shall never see your face again'. She replied: 'Sir, I will take all the care I can that you never shall.' (3)

Writing after the marriage split, William's brother wrote: 'My brother and his wife are parted never to meet again. She was young and indiscreet, he was old and jealous, qualities which by no means agree, and therefore it was much better for them to part.' (4)

Sir William paid her an allowance and she retained her title but was free to make her own life. She retained her attachment to the stage and as already noted she played Calista opposite to Prince Edward, Duke of York's Lothario in The Fair Penitent. She also played in the tragedy of Jane Shore, again with Edward playing Lord Hastings. It was rumoured that she and Edward were in love. They were certainly having an affair but it all ended with his untimely death in Monaco from a fever in September 1767. (5)

Sir William died in 1772, and so Anne was free to marry again. This time she married a man eight years younger than herself, a Captain in the Life Guards, one Charles Morris. Charles was a friend of the Prince of Wales and became known as a writer of political and lyrical songs. There are few references to her after her marriage. Presumably her husband died before her as she died at Melton Constable, the home of the Astley family, in February, 1812. (6)

Rhoda had two daughters called Sarah, the first was born in 1738 and died a few days later. The second Sarah was born in 1742 and was her last child. Sarah grew up at Delaval Hall but was determined to leave and make a good marriage. When she was eighteen, in 1760, she married Sir John Savile, 1st Lord Pollington, who later in 1766 was raised to an earldom as the 1st Earl of Mexborough (7) In 1761 Sarah and her husband attended the coronation of King George III. The occasion was recorded in a picture by Sir Joshua Reynolds now on display at Doddington Hall. John was MP for New Shoreham but because his title was in the Peerage of Ireland he was not given a seat in the House of Lords, so continued to sit as an MP. They lived in the family home at Methley in Yorkshire, but they also had property in London and later they purchased Canon Park, described as a modest country house in the Georgian style, built in 1760. (8) Sarah had three children, John, Henry and Charles. John became the 2nd Earl on his father's death. Besides her own children, Sarah also looked after Frances, the daughter of her brother Francis and Betty Roach. For a while Canon Park was on the social circuit. Prince Edward was seen there along with Samuel Foote, his actor friends, and other members of the Delaval family. Foote organised plays and puppet-shows here as well as less formal forms of entertainment such as sack races. It was also at Canon that Foote had the fall that cost him his leg and very nearly his life. (9)

Sarah, most unfortunately, lent her brother Francis £10,000 and this was never repaid. Probably as a result of this debt the Mexboroughs ended up in financial difficulties themselves and Canon Park was sold. In 1778 John Mexborough died, aged fifty-nine. In 1780 Sarah married the Rev. Stanford Hardcastle, the Rector of Adel in Yorkshire. He died in 1788 and she spent the later part of her life in her house at Dover Street, London. She died in 1821 - the last of her generation of Delavals.

Rhoda also had five sons Robert, George, Henry, Ralph, and Edward. They all left Delaval Hall in the decade 1750-60 and only Edward ever came back. Robert became a soldier and was killed after the capture of Quebec, in 1760. George was said to have been lost at sea before June 1758, and Henry, an army captain, died in India in June 1760. Ralph was a merchant living in Lisbon at the time of the great earthquake in 1755. He was presumed killed (10). No wonder people said that the Delavals were cursed!

Edward, the last of the Delavals, died in 1814. His story is told in chapter thirteen.

Notes on chapter eleven

1. *Lord Chesterfield's letters to his Godson, edited by The Earl of Caernarvon, 1889, p313*

2. *The correspondence of Thomas Gray and William Mason, edited by The Rev. John Mitford, second edtn, 1855, p530*

3. *Walpole's Correspondence, Vol 22, p164*

4. *Lord Chesterfield's letters, p341*

5. *Memoirs of Richard Edgworth, Begun by Himself, Vol. 1 1821, p148*

6. *County History, Vol. IX, p173*

7. *The Gay Delavals, Francis Askham, 1955, p95*

8. *Spelling - some sources say Canon others Cannons*

9. *See chapter 8*

10. *County History, Vol. 1X, p173*

CHAPTER TWELVE
TROUBLESOME CHILDREN

Francis and Sarah Hussey Delaval.

Sir John, and his first wife Susanna, had seven children. The first born was a girl, Rhoda, named after her grandmother and her aunt. Her birth was registered on 18th February 1751. She probably lived for a while in London but after the death of her grandparents, Sir John spent more time at Seaton and Doddington. All we know about Rhoda is to be found in a small bundle o letters preserved in the archives at the Northumberland County Records Office. They are beautifully written in a firm hand. In one of the letters written from Ford Castle, in August 1769, she writes: 'Dear Papa, We were made hay by your dear letter and all extremely rejoiced to hear you are well. We are all in perfect health. I have sent all the newspapers and letters what I have received from Berwick since your departure.

Pray give my love to my dear mama,

Your most dutiful daughter Rhoda' (1)

Her father was then staying with the Duke of Northumberland at Alnwick Castle. Besides affectionate letters to her father there are also some written to a friend in Italian. In August 1770 Rhoda was staying at Doddington, where sadly she died, probably of consumption, at the age of just nineteen. The church at Doddington was in such a poor state of repair that Rhoda could not be buried inside, and so her grave is outside in the churchyard. Sir John was so concerned about the state of the church that he wrote to the Bishop of Lincoln and then set about its repair.

Sir John's second daughter, Susanna, died when she was eleven in October 1764. Very little is known about her.

Sir John's only son, John, died tragically young and some of his letters are also preserved in the archives. Young John, often referred to as Jack, was a weak, sickly child who was educated at home. One of his tutors was the Rev. Thomas Hall, brother-in-law to the Methodist preachers, John and Charles Wesley. Hall was a scholarly gentleman who knew Mr. Potter, Susannah's first husband, hence his introduction to the Delavals. He was not on good terms with the Wesley brothers as he had fallen out with them over his marriage to their sister. Charles Wesley came to visit Seaton Sluice in 1764 to preach from the glass works steps. Of Delaval Hall, he wrote: 'The front is remarkable noble. In the house I saw nothing remarkable but was remarkable bad.' (2) If we look at extracts from the childrens' letters, we can see that Jack's letters are written in a thin spidery hand. (3) They are untidy with alterations and crossings out, very different from the neat confident letters of his sisters. In a letter written in 1770, when he was about fourteen, he tells his father what he had been learning that day: 'Dear Mama and Papa, I have been much entertained with my geography and have been making the grand tour of Europe. We have visited the several cities which I will write under. Mr. Hall thinks it is very necessary to know the principle cities and different countries such as Paris in France.' He goes on to make a list of countries and cities then says: 'I will conclude with the utmost reverence, your ever affectionate, John Hussey Delaval.' Some letters asking for favours often have a cringing, whinging tone, about them. In one letter to his father he asks: 'If you would let me write three times a week instead of every night' (4). John wanted to know what he was doing, however as so few letters have survived it seems Jack got his way.

John 'Jack' Delaval, the last male heir of the Delavals.

Jack appears to have had a difficult relationship with his father. John was probably disappointed in him, as this weak, sickly boy, with an eye for servant girls, was not what he hoped for as the heir to the Delaval empire. It all ended tragically in July 1775 while staying at Hot Springs in Bristol. Jack had gone there to treat his consumption and supposedly, according to tradition, he was molesting a servant girl when she kicked him in the crotch and he subsequently died of his injuries. He was buried inside the Church at Doddington. His father in a mixture of rage and grief had the interior of the church painted black for the service. He had an obituary notice published in the Morning Post part of which read: 'John whose death is grievously lamented by his most afflicted parents, and by all who had the happiness of being acquainted with him. His manners were so pure, unaffected, and amiable, and his behaviour so engaging and irresistible, that he captivated the affections, and was the delight of all that knew him.' (5) Shortly after Jack's death Sir John had a Mausoleum built at Seaton Delaval. It cost £1742 11s 0d, and was to have been a memorial to his son but it was never consecrated and so never used. It was said that the Bishop of Durham demanded too high a fee to come and consecrate the building.

Jack's death meant that John could not leave the Delaval empire to his family. His mother's will was drawn up in such a way that Doddington could not be left to his daughters, but had to go to his brother Edward. Similarly the Seaton Estate would have to go to the male grandchildren of his sister Rhoda, who would take precedence over his daughters. Sadly John had fallen out with Edward over Doddington and they never were friends again.

Sophia Anne, Sir John's third daughter, was baptised in January 1755. A portrait by William Bell shows her wearing a yellow gown with lace around the neck. She has light brown hair and a rather vacant expression. She spent her childhood at Seaton and Doddington with her brother and sisters. When she was about twenty one she went to Europe and became involved with a Mr Devereux of Bordeaux. In 1778 she returned to England, pregnant, but with no sign of Mr Devereux. She went to Doddington where she gave birth to a boy. His birth is recorded in the church register as follows: 'Henry son of Henry Devereux of Burdeux in France by Sophia Delaval.' (6) Then Delaval was crossed out and Devereux written above it.

Leaving behind her a trail of unpaid bills, which her long - suffering father reluctantly settled, Sophia returned to France. A year later she returned to England with a husband, not Mr Devereux, but a Mr John Godfrey Maximilian Jadis, a gentleman she had met in Ghent and supposedly married in the Catholic Cathedral in Brussels. Sir John immediately contacted his lawyer, Mr Farrer, and told him to find out who this Mr Jadis was. Farrer investigated and found that Jadis was indeed an ensign in the 59th Regiment of Foot, as he claimed. John told Farrer to arrange a proper marriage as soon as possible, as he did not want any more illegitimate children in the family. So they were duly married on the 6th February 1780, at St. Mary's Lambeth.

Sir John made them an allowance of £500 per year and they rented a house near Leatherhead in Surrey for £36 p.a. Eventually Sophia brought her new husband to meet the family at Seaton. Here, John's favourite daughter Sarah, who had married Lord Tyrconnel, held court. Sophia, with a penniless ensign for her husband, could hardly be considered to have made a good match.

Mr Jadis did not fit in and ended up quarrelling with Lord Tyrconnel and challenging him to a duel. Sir John ensured there wouldn't be any fighting and virtually threw Jadis out. Sophia, banished from Seaton, lived with her husband for about six years, then they parted in a flurry of debt and recriminations. Sir John agreed to pay Jadis £100 a year to keep him quiet, and there is letter from Jadis to John dated 12th June 1792 in which Jadis writes: 'My Lord, The only return I can make your Lordships kind attention to me is my most sincere

Elizabeth, Lady Audley (1753-1785) by William Bell, 1774.

thanks and I shall always make it to my merit the patronage you have so kindly bestowed.' (7) The letter does not make it clear what John had done but he had probably paid off creditors. Meanwhile Sophia like many a troubled soul, turned to opium. She died in 1793 leaving unpaid drugs bills for £96. The last we hear of Jadis is in a letter from a gentleman in Devon in 1799 asking Sir John to pay debts of: 'a person who stiles him self as your son in law by name John Godfrey Maximillian Jadis.' (8) He then apparently went to Nova Scotia. Meanwhile Sophia's young son was brought up by his grandmother at Seaton. Harry Jadis, as he was known, proved to be a popular boy and even Sir John grew to like him.

John had three other daughters, Elizabeth, Frances and Sarah. All of them have left letters written by themselves, and in all the letters written when they were children, the style is very deferential and show that the children quickly learned how to flatter their parents and to write letters to please them.

In December 1772, Elizabeth wrote from her father's London home at Milbank to The Author of The London Evening Post: 'Sir, A partie quaree, consisting of two Royal Princes and their amiable consorts, having agreed to pass an evening in writing some little productions of wit, you here receive the genuine performance of her Royal Highness the Duchess of Cumberland a strong proof that her pregnant wit is not inferior to her high station. I am your humble servant. Elizabeth Delaval' (9) This extraordinary invitation shows that the Delavals were close friends of the Duke and Duchess of Cumberland, indeed they were frequent visitors to Cumberland House. The Duke of Cumberland, the brother of King George III, had married a daughter of Simon Lutterel who was known as the biggest reprobate in England. This marriage so outraged the King that he refused to see his brother or anyone associating with him, so Sir John and Lady Delaval were informed that they could not be received at court. However Sir John remained friends with the Duke who visited Delaval Hall in 1771.

In May 1781, Elizabeth married George Thicknesse, Baron Audley. George inherited the title from his mother's family and it brought him an income of £2,000 per year. His father Philip Thicknesse deeply resented his son's elevation to the peerage and publicly conspired against him, accusing him of seducing the daughter of a clergyman. This naturally upset the newly married couple, but their marriage survived and over the next four years they had three children. In November 1782 Elizabeth wrote to her father: 'Dear Papa, Thank you for your letter I am much obliged to you for enclosed draught. I have the happiness to acquaint you and My dear mama that my sweet little girl has cut a tooth and is perfectly well and in very great spirit. To my dear papa your ever dutiful and affectionate daughter Elizabeth Audley.

Received from JHD the sum of £250 for my half year increase due to me from 21st May -21st Nov1782.' (10) The receipt of their allowance prompted many letters of thanks from John's daughters. In the summer of 1785 Elizabeth became ill and she died on the 11th July, aged 27. She was the fourth of John's children to die.

Frances, John's fifth daughter, was born in March 1759 at Seaton. Like her sisters she was taught to read and write and as she grew up she spent time in each of the Delaval houses. If we look at her letters we can see that she writes a very neat hand taking great care over each letter. In the extract from her letter written at Grosvenor House, London, in 1793, writing to one of her sisters, she enquires after the health of her parents and her brother.

In August 1778, Frances married John Fenton of Lancaster, who, in 1781, inherited a modest estate at Wyreside in Lancashire, and became Mr Fenton Cawthorne.

John

My Dear Father & Mother,

as it is allways my aim to deserve your approbation I hope that the request which I am going to make will not offend you, I am

Elizabeth

My Dear Papa & mama Grovesnor ... 31 1770

as you have been so good as to let me learn Italian I hope

Frances

My Dear sister,

I hope my dear Mamma is quite recoverd and had no return of her illness in her way to Sion; you will give my Duty to my dear Papa, and

Sarah

my dear mamma

I am very much ashamed of my behavour to day and do deserve to be punished I will not desire to read another book till tusday or longer and only wish

Examples of hand writing by the children of Sir John Delaval.

Shortly after their marriage they went on a continental tour where they probably met up with sister Sophia. When they returned, John unsuccessfully stood for the parliamentary election in Preston. In 1783 he tried again in Lincoln and this time was elected as their MP. He supported the Fox-North Coalition, and his father-in-law, Sir John. When Sir John switched sides and supported William Pitt, his son-in-law defended him in a speech in Parliament. All seemed to be going well until 1790, when new elections were held. John again stood for Lincoln. At first it appeared that the election would be uncontested but unfortunately this was not to be. Three candidates contested the election and John Fenton Cawthorne had a fight on his hands.

He came to Seaton and it seems that Sir John gave him £300 to fight the election. William Portes, John's agent at Doddington, wrote to Sir John saying he had never seen Lincoln so crowded with people and that all three candidates had been walking the streets with colours flying. It was the most hotly contested election for years. When the result was announced John Cawthorne headed the poll - not so surprising since he had spent £2,500 to win the seat!

Sir John was annoyed when he heard how much the election had cost and enraged when he found it had all been charged to his account. There followed a typical Delaval Family row over money. Sir John at first refused to pay anything but when it became obvious that the creditors would go to law and that with legal fees the final bill would be nearer £5,000, he paid up.

However Sir John was determined Cawthorne would repay the money, he forced him to sell assets and he cut Frances's allowance. Having spent a fortune to get into parliament Cawthorne did very little when he got there. He supported Pitt but he made very few interventions in debates. Burdened by debt from the Lincoln election, he joined the army as a Colonel in the Westminster Regiment but his pay of £1 2s 6d a day did little to reduce his debts. As part of his duties he looked after the regimental funds and the temptation to use these funds to solve his financial problems proved too much. He took money due to his men for himself, and he raided the regimental funds. Taking money from army funds was not unusual in the corrupt army of the time and he was merely reprimanded. However his corrupt ways continued and eventually he was court-martialled on fourteen charges. Among these charges were recommending men for service who were not fit and keeping their pay for himself, promoting boys who were too young to serve as ensigns and keeping their pay and taking bribes. He was found guilty on eleven of the charges against him and was sentenced to be cashiered and declared unworthy to serve his Majesty ever again. In May 1796, the House of Commons voted that he should be expelled and his crimes recorded in the Journals of the House.

Throughout all this scandal and shame Frances stayed with her husband. After her sister Sarah's death in October 1800, she was the only daughter still alive. In 1801 she appears to be back in touch with her father because in a letter dated 15th July she writes about the weather and her garden and concludes: 'You would be astonished to see the quantity of grapes, but I now despair ever having the happiness of receiving you. It is a long while since we have met all together.' (11) The letter is signed FFC. Gone is the neat writing of her youth and it is difficult to read in places. After the garden news the real purpose of the letter and her pain is revealed in the last lines. In another letter to her father she tells him they are due to receive four thousand pounds and goes on to say this will be good news for Cawthorne. (12)

However after some debt repayment and passing of time Frances seems reconciled with her father. She writes in a letter dated 17th June 1807: 'My Dearest Papa, I return my best thanks for the draft of £125 which I have duly received. I am very happy and thankful to find that you are recovered from your cold. I sincerely hope you are now perfectly well, and that Lady Delaval is also well. Mr Cawthorne proposes to set out to town in a few days on business.

He joins me in love to yourself and our dear lady Delaval and I remain my dearest Papa you most aff. and Dutiful Daughter F F Cawthorne.' (13)

Sir John died the next year in 1808. Frances lived on into the Victorian era and died in 1839 - the last of her generation of Delavals.

Sir John's favourite daughter was his youngest, Sarah Hussey. She was born 1st July 1763 and was usually called Hussey or Miss Hussey. From an early age she learnt how to manipulate her parents. She was the only person able to influence Sir John. The best looking of the girls, she had a bewitching charm. A portrait painted when she was about eight shows her in a stiff white dress with pale golden hair, already an assured beauty. 'I can always get what I want from Papa she announced.' (14)

At fifteen she could be seen riding round the estate on a stallion so spirited no one else dare ride him. She was about sixteen when she first caught the attention of Frederick, the Duke of York and Albany. The second son of King George III, he was born in 1763 and so was the same age as Sarah. She wrote to her mother from London mentioning the very marked attention she had received from the Duke. Sir John, sensing the havoc that his wild but beautiful daughter could cause, quickly married her off to his old friend, George Carpenter, 2nd Earl Tyrconnel. (1750-1805) (15)

They were married on the 3rd June 1780 and spent their honeymoon at Doddington where Sarah insisted they played Blind Man's Bluff and showed off the beautiful diamonds her husband had given her as a wedding present. The Duke of York meanwhile went with the army to the continent spending most of the next seven years abroad. Sarah and her husband spent much time at Seaton particularly after the death of Lady Delaval.

After Frederick Duke of York returned to England in 1787 he sought out Sarah, now the mother of two young children, and within three months they were lovers. Wraxall in his Memoirs writes that Sarah was: 'Feminine and delicate in her figure, very fair with a profusion of light hair, in the tresses of which, like the tangles of Neaera's in "Lycides", His Royal Highness (The Duke of York) was detained captive.' Meanwhile Sir John bought Claremont, a country house near Esher in Surrey, to provide a country retreat for his daughter and husband. In July 1788 the Duke of York bought Oatlands, which was according to Walpole: 'very near Claremont House the seat of Lord Tyrconnel whose wife was so notoriously the Dukes mistress.' (16)

Soon the Duke and Sarah were seen out together walking in Vauxhall Pleasure Gardens in the late evening with Sarah wearing little more than a white chemise tied with a blue bow and her hair hanging in ringlets to her waist. Lord Tyrconnel, who had his own outside interests, was quite relaxed about the situation, while Sir John was positively proud of the affair. The Duke held a party for his birthday at Oatlands and he invited his neighbours from Claremont. Sarah and the whole company danced till dawn. The only person affronted by the affair was Mrs Fitzherbert, the 'wife' of The Prince of Wales, the Duke's brother. She refused to receive Sarah on the grounds she was 'contaminate'. A cartoon produced by James Aitken in 1789, shows Lord Tyrconnel leaving the bedroom and wishing the Duke of York goodnight as he is climbing into bed where a bare-breasted Sarah is waiting for him. (see page 79) (17)

Claremont House, described as elegant rather than grand, contained banqueting rooms, water-closets, a powdering room and even a bathroom. (18) It provided a convenient meeting place for the family. Sarah was a charming hostess, Lord Tyrconnel was relaxed and enjoyed a game of cards in the evening, and Sir John,who paid the bills, could bring Miss Hicks. Sarah's two children could play with the sadly motherless Audley trio and young Harry Jadis would be there as well. In 1790 Sarah's first child died leaving her with only one child, her daughter Susan, and the Duke went on to marry Princess Frederika of Prussia. This marriage, like most royal marriages of the time, was a disaster; a dull German Princess was no substitute for the captivating Lady Tyrconnel.

At the end of 1790 Seaton Delaval Hall went 'En Fete' when The Delavals presented ' The Fair Penitent'. The family as usual played the parts.

Lady Tyrconnel played the part of Calista, the lonely and faithless wife who, repenting of her adultery, stabs herself on her lover's bier, a gesture the audience appreciated. The Newcastle Chronicle enthused about the performance: 'Language cannot describe the bewitching charms of the beautiful Calista. The most perfect judgement, taste and elegance characterise this amiable and accomplished female who is the darling of her family.' (19) The theatre was erected in the hall and afterwards the guests were treated to a huge banquet.

The play was repeated in February 1791 and this performance was seen by Henry Swinburne of Hamsterley Hall near Gibside. He noted: 'Lord Delaval was correct and pathetic. Lady Tyrconnel now and then mumbled her phrase, but looked the thing.' After the play came: 'a strange farce written by Williams and Spearman … it was beyond any thing I ever saw or heard of: such a farrago of officers, nuns, lovers, conjurers; ancient and modern times and manners all jumbled together hodge-podge.' After the entertainment the hundred or more guests adjourned to the saloon for: 'a magnificent supper with abundance of wines. There were some clever songs and then dancing and card parties till the morning.' (20) Some days later Swinburne was having dinner with his friend John, the 10th Earl of Strathmore at Gibside, his County Durham estate. He was fascinated by his friend's account of his evening with the eccentric Delavals and asked if he could obtain a ticket for the next performance. Swinburne did so and took him to Delaval Hall. The Earl was just twenty-two, handsome, single and rich. When he had taken over the Gibside Estate from his mother it was despoiled and neglected and the old house was in need of repair. At Delaval Hall the young Earl was overwhelmed by the happy atmosphere there and captivated by Sarah's performance. He fell instantly in love with her and within weeks the attraction was returned and they became inseparable. The satirists of the time noted the change of partners. Isaac Cruikshank produced a cartoon showing Lord Strathmore hiding under Sarah's bed as the Duke of York enters the room. In fact the affair with the Duke of York was over before Sarah became involved with Lord Strathmore. (21) These cartoons were meant to be humorous but they also often exposed the hypocrisy and pomposity of the ruling classes.

In 1792 Strathmore bought Claremont Lodge which was about a mile from Claremont House. Here, he stabled some of his thorough-bred race horses and Lord Strathmore and the amenable Lord Tyrconnel became racing partners. Back at Seaton the family staged what proved to be their last major production,

Othello. Sir John played the noble Moor of Venice; Lady Tyrconnel played Desdemona; Lord Tyrconnel was the villain, Iago, and Lord Strathmore the innocent, Cassio.

Hundreds of candles lit up the Hall and gardens, immense quantities of food were provided and dozens of bottles of claret, port, sherry, Madeira and brandy were available for the guests who took supper in the saloon. Although not realised at the time, it was a fitting end to flamboyant Delaval theatricals. The decline in the Delaval fortune and shortages caused by the war with France made it impossible to put on such a show of over-consumption again.

When they were in the North, Sarah and Strathmore lived openly at Gibside and if there was horse racing there she would proudly present the cups. She was said once to have danced naked to the waist to entertain the entranced officers at a regimental ball at Gibside. In 1795 the Duke of York, as head of the British army, brought 7,000 troops to exercise on Blyth beach. Why did he choose the Beach between Seaton Sluice and Blyth? Could it have been because he knew Sarah would be in the vicinity? Thousands of people went to watch the spectacle but there is no evidence that Sarah did. She was now only interested in John Strathmore, and they continued their life together at Claremont and Gibside. The easy going Lord Tyrconnel found his position becoming intolerable and when Sir John heard that Sarah was thinking of marrying Strathmore he firmly forbade it. (22) No doubt this came as a shock to Sarah as she was used to getting her own way.

As the decade progressed Sarah had other things to think about. Her health began to deteriorate and in 1798 it became clear that she was not well. She tried various pills and potions. A letter written by her daughter in July 1800 shows that she had changed her diet and lifestyle. Susan writes: ' she never tastes either animal food, malt liquor or wine but dines and sups on vegetables and fruit. She also indulges in a little gentle horse exercise and inhales ether and drinks asses milk.' (23) However nothing worked and as the long hot summer rolled on it became obvious she was ill. At Seaton, Dr Abbs treated her for consumption with digitalis and thought she would recover. By September she had gone to Gibside and here she was visited by George Ocheltrie. He wrote to Sir John who was at Ford Castle as follows: 'Sep. 26th 1800 My Lord I have just arrived from Gibside, where I have been for two days ….I left her ladyship in good spirits and she finds herself a great deal better since she went there, the winds being so variable had an impressive effect upon her ladyship so near the sea at Seaton Delaval, I trust in God the change In air will answer the desired purpose.' (24). Alas it was not to be. Neither digitalis nor a change of air could save Sarah.

She died on the 7th October 1800, at Gibside. An obituary notice appeared in the Newcastle Chronicle a few days later obviously written by her father: 'Died Tuesday last at Seaton Delaval, inconsolably lamented by her family and deeply regretted by all who knew her, the Countess of Tyrconnel after a severe illness of many months which she bore with such patience and resignation as could only have been supported by her inimitable suavity of temper and the truest sense of religion.' (25) Sir John was trying to hide the fact that she died at the home of her lover. Of course the obituary fooled no-one. The Gentleman's Magazine bluntly stated that she died at Gibside. John Strathmore gave her a funeral which nearly ruined the estate, then she was buried in Westminster Abbey after a very odd service. According to the Gentleman's Magazine: 'The remains of the Countess of Tyrconnel were deposited in great funeral pomp. Her nephew was the only person related who followed her to the grave, the rest of the mourners consisted of her principle domestics. Her ladyship was in the 36th year of her age and she died at Gibside. She had been on a visit to his lordship having left her father's house in Portland Place only a fortnight before. The cause of death is supposed to have been a violent cold caught on her journey.' (26)

Why were no close family at the service in the Abbey? Why was she going up and down to London if she was dying from consumption? George Ocheltrie's letter written ten days before she died says she was 'in good spirits' - no mention of a cold. Her father's account of her last days is at odds with the other account and we know he was lying over her death at Gibside!

Sarah made a lasting impression on all who knew her. She was described as 'bewitching' and Dean Stanley referred to her as: 'the wildest of her race.' (27) John Strathmore adored her and was said to be broken-hearted. Yet he went to Seaton Delaval where he began an ill- judged affair with Sarah's 19 year old daughter, Lady Susan Carpenter, who was just as indulged and spoilt as her mother had been. John did eventually propose to her and at first she accepted his proposal. To give herself some time to consider her position she went to stay with her aunt, Frances.

Lord Tyrconnel, her father, was against the match, the affair waned and so they never married. To give his daughter some independence her father gave her an income of £800 a year and his town house.

In 1805 Lady Susan did marry, not Lord Strathmore, but Henry de la Poer-Beresford, 2nd Marquis of Waterford. When Sir John died in 1808 he left Ford Castle and the Royal Northumberland Bottle Works to his wife for her lifetime, and then it was to go to his granddaughter Lady Susan. (28)

Lord Strathmore meanwhile, returned to Gibside and his beloved thorough-bred racehorses. Here, he began an affair with Mary Milner, a beautiful girl, the daughter of a market gardener from Stainton, and for the next twenty years he lived with Mary as his wife. In 1820, when he knew he was dying, he married her at a special ceremony, where one of the witnesses was Henry Jadis who had become a close friend. John Strathmore died the next morning and was buried in the Chapel at Gibside. (29)

With the death of Sarah, Claremont House was no longer needed so Sir John sold it for £55,000. One other point of interest in the family correspondence is the little matter of the return of the diamonds that Lord Tyrconnel had given to Sarah as a wedding present. Eventually the gems were located and returned to Lord Tyrconnel. Sarah, Lady Tyrconnel will perhaps be remembered for being the mistress of the Duke of York but she wasn't the only family member to be involved with the Royal Family. Her aunt, on her husband's side, Lady Almeria, had for many years been the favourite of the Duke of Gloucester. (30) Uncle Francis had been a firm friend to a previous Duke of York and so had Lady Stanhope! Sir John was a friend of the Duke of Cumberland until his death in 1790. For a small landed family from the remote North of England, the Delavals proved remarkably adept at social climbing.

Notes on chapter twelve

1. *Document County Record Office, DP 0429/18/20*

2. *The Journal of John Wesley, Editor J Curnock, 1909, p29 and The Delaval Papers, p34.*

3. *C.R.O. 2 DE /39/2/9*

4. *C.R.O. 2DE/39/2/6*

5. *The Gay Delavals p166*

6. *ibid p175*

7. *C.R.O. 2DE 39/5/13*

8. *The Gay Delavals p245*

9. *Walpole's Correspondence, Vol 36, p84*

10. *C.R.O. 2DE39/6*

11. *C.R.O. 2DE39/10/21*

12. *The £4,000 mentioned in letter 2DE/39/10/19 appears to have been paid five years later after disputed legal proceedings*

13. C.R.O. 2DE39/10/29

14. The Unhappy Countess, Ralph Arnold, p157

15. The Diaries of a Duchess, p 46. Sarah was Tyrconnel's second wife. His first wife was Frances Manners, daughter of the Marquis of Granby

16. Walpole's Correspondence, Vol 42, p472

17. Lord Tyrconnel had several affairs. In a series of letters one of his mistresses signed herself EB. CRO 2DE/39/21/27

18. Daily Life in England in The Reign of George III, p24
The Claremont estate was originally laid out by Vanbrugh, then the house was replaced by one designed by Lancelot 'Capability' Brown and Henry Holland in 1774.

19. Gibside and The Bowes Family, p 80. The Newcastle Chronicle 15th January 1791, reported that Lady Tyrconnel attended a performance of The Provok'd Husband by Vanbrugh, followed by a farce and other entertainments at The North Shields Theatre.

20. The Courts of Europe by Swinburne, p99

21. City of Laughter, p343

22. C.R.O. 2DE/39/13/16

23. Durham County Records Office Strathmore Collection D/ST C1/12/1

24. C.R.O. 2DE39/25/9

25. The Gay Delavals, p222

26. The Gentleman's Magazine, 1800, Vol. 2, p1104

27. The Gay Delavals p221

28. County History, p165

29. The Unhappy Countess p164

30. Portraits of the Duke of Gloucester and Lady Almeria face each other at Kiplin Hall, near Richmond

CHAPTER THIRTEEN
EDWARD HUSSEY DELAVAL F.R.S.
1729-1814

Edward was the third son of Rhoda and Captain Francis Blake Delaval. A year younger than John, he was baptised at Newburn Parish Church on 18th June 1729, having been born at his grandparents' house at South Dissington. (1) Said to be rather a timid child, he proved himself an able scholar and was the only Delaval to have a good academic school record. He played only small parts in the Delaval theatrical productions but like all the family he loved the theatre.

He was affectionately known by the family as Ned.

At the age of eighteen, in July 1747, he went to Pembroke College, Cambridge, and his name appears in the Cambridge calendar as having taken a first class degree in mathematical tripos, 1750-51 (2). While at Pembroke, Edward became friends with the poet Thomas Gray, whose work includes 'Elegy Written in a Country Churchyard' and 'Ode on a Distant Prospect of Eton College.' Gray also wrote a number of letters to friends and it is through these letters that we can trace Edward's career through Pembroke College. Of Edward's degree he writes: 'Delaval, a fellow commoner (a younger son of old Delaval of Northumberland), who has taken a degree in an exemplary manner and is very sensible and knowing.'(3) Edward was elected as a Fellow of Pembroke College in 1751 and spent much of the next ten years there. He was at ease with college life and was an able scholar. That Gray knew Edward quite well is evident from the tone of the letters in which he sometimes refers to Edward as Marcello, a secret nickname or simply as Delly. He describes Edward as having a booming voice and on more than one occasion calls him 'Delaval the Loud'.

Edward was awarded his M.A. in 1754. He became a scientist of note and distinguished himself in the study of chemistry and experimental philosophy. In 1759 he became a member of the Royal Society, one of his proposers being Benjamin Franklin, with whom he had been in correspondence concerning lightning conductors. They were both members of a committee appointed by the Dean and Chapter of St. Paul's Cathedral to recommend ways to protect the cathedral from a lightning strike. The subject of electricity was of great interest to him; he was in favour of blunt lightning conductors and published his observations in 1773. (4) Edward made sure that Delaval Hall was one of the first buildings in the country to have a lightning conductor fitted.

Edward's party piece was playing the musical glasses. Gray writes to his friend the Rev. James Brown: 'we heard Delaval the other night play upon the water glasses, and I was astonished. No other instrument that I know has so celestial a tone.' (5) Writing to his friend, and fellow poet, William Mason, he said: 'for here is Mr Delaval and a charming set of glasses that sing like nightingales and we have concerts every other night.' (6)

In 1762 Edward was considered for a professorship 'Next to myself', wrote Gray: 'I wish it for him (Delaval).' In fact neither of them succeeded. Curiously Edward got support from an unexpected source, his brother Francis using his position as a member of parliament asked the Duke of Newcastle to write to Lord Egremont at Cambridge, recommending Edward for the post of professor of modern history. In those more relaxed days such posts were largely sinecures requiring very little work from the holder. Francis also used his position in Parliament to support the administration led by Lord Bute in the hope of securing a favour for his favourite brother. When Edward did not get the post Francis considered he had been badly let down. (7) When later that year the new Prime Minister, George Grenville, wrote to Francis inviting him to the opening of Parliament, Francis replied with a long, scathing letter.

'Downing Street 24th Oct 1763,

Sir- I have received your letter, in which you are pleased to say that many of my friends hope to see me in town. I should be glad to know who my friends are, having never in this Administration been able to find one.'

The letter went on complaining about the way his small request had been treated by the administration. Grenville replied the same day asking Francis to go and see him. As a result of this meeting a pension of £300 a year appears against the name of Edward Delaval, in a secret service list, drawn up in 1764. It was probably paid until he died, and a mollified Francis voted with the government on parliamentary business. (8)

Meanwhile Edward continued his scientific work. In 1765 he read a paper to the Royal Society: 'containing experiments and observations on the agreement between the specific gravities of the several metals, and their colours when united to glass.' In 1766 he was one of the joint winners of The Copley Medal, then the highest award of the Royal Society for this work. In 1774 he conducted a series of experiments upon phosphorus and the colours produced by it in the dark. He published a paper in 1777 entitled: 'An experimental inquiry into the cause of the changes of colours in opake and coloured bodies, with an historical preface.' (9) He was also noted for his work on producing artificial gemstones. Several of his papers were translated into French and Italian, and he corresponded with various continental students and scientists. The Royal Societies of Upsal and Gottingen, and the Institute of Bologna, enrolled him amongst their members. He was also an honorary member of the Literary and Philisophical Society of Newcastle. Besides his scientific work, he was a noted classical scholar, was conversant in several modern languages and was an accurate judge of art and music. He also maintained the reputation of the family for giving charity to the poor and benevolence to local institutions.

In 1768, Gray notes that: 'Delaval is by no means well, and looks sadly, yet he goes about and talks as loudly as ever.' (10) Later that year he married Sarah, daughter of George Scott, and they took up residence in a neat house in Parliament Place, London. Here the leading scientists of the day mixed with poets like Gray and Mason. (11). When his brother Francis died in 1771 Edward should have been able to take over Doddington Hall, but John refused to give it up. Under the terms of their mother's will Doddington and Seaton could not be owned by the same person. A long and bitter legal battle followed, but eventually a settlement was reached between them. John kept Doddington but paid an annual rent to Edward. It wasn't until after John's death that Edward was able to move into Doddington.

When John died in 1808, his second wife, Susanna, was left the Ford Estate and the Bottle Works. Edward inherited Seaton Delaval Hall, Hartley and Doddington. Under the terms of his mother's will, other family members, such as Lady Stanhope, had a minority interest in Doddington. Edward bought them out so he could leave the estate to his wife and daughter. He had no desire to visit Seaton Delaval Hall again due to his advanced age and because he knew it would have to go to the Astley family on his death, so he sent instructions that some of the best pictures and fittings be removed and sent to Doddington. These were loaded on board ships and sent by sea, river and canal to Doddington. Although Edward didn't know it at the time, he had done a very good thing - for he saved these valuable artefacts from the fire of 1822. One of the pictures he saved was that of his brother Francis by Sir Joshua Reynolds. Edward added to the beauty of Doddington in other ways. He replanted the trees that John had ruthlessly chopped down and laid out the fish pond. Edward put a caretaker in charge of Delaval Hall, a Mr. Samuel Huthwaite. (12) Delaval Hall slept quietly through the twilight years of the Delaval family, the only disturbances being caused by the occasional poacher.

Edward and his wife had one daughter, Sarah. In April 1805 she married a wealthy gentleman from Dover, a Mr James Gunman, who was 25 years her senior. Edward gave Doddington to Sarah and her husband to live in. The Gunmans were a distinguished naval family and some pictures on the stairs at Doddington celebrate the heroics of Captain Christopher Gunman.

Edward lived on at his 'neat gothic house in Parliament Place,'(13) where some parts of the interior were elegantly formed of artificial stone, which he had invented. He died at the ripe old age of 85 on the 14th August 1814, and was buried in Westminster Abbey. Edward was the last of his generation. The last male Delaval. As there were no surviving male children the estate at Seaton passed to the grandchild of Rhoda Apreece who had married Captain Francis Blake Delaval. Her daughter, also Rhoda, had married Edward Astley of Melton Constable back in 1751 and it was her son, Sir Jacob Astley, who inherited the estate. So after seven hundred years the Delaval name died out and Seaton Delaval Hall became the property of the Astley Family.

Edward had left his London property to his wife who survived until 1829, and his daughter Sarah inherited Doddington. In 1825, Sarah's husband, James, died. She became involved with a Mr. George Jarvis, and for a while it seemed they would marry, but sadly Sarah died of consumption in May 1825. Although she never married him she left Doddington to George Jarvis, who took possession on the death of Lady Delaval in 1829. His descendants still own the property.

Edward had lived a quiet and sober life, he was a noted scholar and his death was mourned by members of the scientific community both here and on the continent.

Notes on chapter thirteen

1. *The Dissington branch of the family were past patrons of Newburn Parish Church*

2. *The Correspondence of Thomas Gray and William Mason, edited by The Rev. J. Mitford, 1855, p55*

3. *ibid, p27*

4. *An Historical and Descriptive View of Northumberland by Mackenzie 1825, p424*

5. *The Correspondence of Thomas Gray etc; p203*

6. *Ibid p283. Musical glasses are a set of glasses each filled with a liquid to a different level. Each glass plays a different note when struck or rubbed.*

7. *The House of Commons 1745-1790 by Napier and Brooke,Vol 2, p309*

8. *The Grenville Papers,Vol 11, p145. A senior member of the administration was given the task of paying out these 'secret' pensions. Some of these secret account books have survived showing money was paid to a wide variety of people for reasons ranging from bribery to simple charity.*

9. *Mackenzie, p424*

10. *The Correspondence of Thomas Gray etc. p412*

11. *Edward probably married Sarah in 1768 but there was some doubt as to the legality of this marriage so he remarried in 1808.*

12. *The Gay Delavals, p236*

13. *The Monthly Chronicle of North-Country Lore and Legend, p255*

CHAPTER FOURTEEN
FIRE AND FAREWELL

The death of Edward, the last legitimate male Delaval, marked the end of seven hundred years of Delaval occupation of Seaton. Their legacy was Seaton Delaval Hall. Although now owned by Sir Jacob Henry Astley (1756-1817) the Hall remained essentially a monument to the Delavals. The Astley Family had their own life in Norfolk and rarely visited Seaton. They retained the Seaton estate but Sir Jacob sold off the remains of the Dissington estate to Edward Collingwood in 1822. Over the centuries other groups of Delavals had formed separate branches of the family. At some time there had been a Tynemouth branch and a Durham branch of the family. Neither of these branches survived for more than a generation or two and by 1800 they had died out. (1)

From 1808 Delaval Hall was looked after by a Mr Huthwaite and his wife, Frances. Samuel Huthwaite came from the Midlands. He was well educated and went to work for an uncle in London. However this didn't work out, so he went to Gateshead to work for another uncle who was a druggist or chemist. Samuel was soon handling a variety of exotic goods and he supplied the Delavals with a wide range of things including beeswax for the glassworks, seeds for the garden, colours for paints and so on. He probably met the Delavals through his wife, Frances. She was an illegitimate daughter of Sir Francis Blake Delaval and Mrs Davison. Her baptism was recorded at St Mary's Church, Gateshead, on September 1st, 1755. The document names her father as Francis Delaval, but her mother wasn't named. In his will, Francis acknowledges four children. One was his natural daughter " Frances, now residing with her grandmother, Mrs Clark at Gateshead." What happened to her mother is not known. Frances grew up in Gateshead. On December 22nd, 1776, the Newcastle Journal reported that Frances "a sprightly lady with a large fortune", married Mr Huthwaite, an eminent chemist in Gateshead. (1A)

When Sir John died in 1808, Edward became the owner of Delaval Hall but he had no desire to live there, so he asked the Huthwaite's to live there instead. Edward removed some family treasure from the Hall but there were many items of furniture, family portraits and boxes of Sir John's papers left in the Hall. Apart from looking after the Hall, Huthwaite's other concern was the prevention of poaching. An order signed in the name of Edward Delaval in 1813 said "all poachers and unqualified persons found trespassing... will be prosecuted with utmost rigour." (2) The game according to contemporary accounts had been "much destroyed."

When Edward died, the Astley's inherited Delaval Hall but they didn't want to live there so the Huthwaite's continued in residence until they died. Samuel passed away on September 1st, 1816 and Frances died in December 1818 in lodgings in Newcastle where she had gone to seek medical advice. Both Samuel and Frances are buried in St Alban's Church at Earsdon.

One could argue that the Huthwaites were the last of the Delavals - only a question of legitimacy deprived them of the honour.

While the Huthwaites occupied Delaval Hall, Lady Delaval, (sir John's second wife) lived in Ford Castle. She was comfortably off. Besides Ford, Sir John had left her the bottle works and an income of £1,000 per year for her life. On her death the Ford Estate was to go to his granddaughter, Susan Carpenter. In 1805 Susan had married the Marquis of Waterford and gone to live at her husband's property in Ireland. Susanna lived a quiet life at Ford but in 1822 she became ill and seeking medical advice she went to the spa town of Matlock. She stayed at the Old Bath Hotel where she died in August. She is buried in St Giles Church, Matlock. An alabster memorial tablet set in the wall states "Here lie the Mortal remains of Susanna Elizabeth Relic of John Hussey Delaval, Baron Delaval, of Seaton Delaval and Ford Castle in the county of Northumberland. She departed this life at Matlock, aged 59."

Susanna left her personal estate to her brother who lived in Rothbury. He is buried in the Parish Church there.

On the death of Lady Delaval in 1822, the Waterfords took formal possession of Ford Castle, and its estate of 7,145 acres. John's other grandchildren appear to have been neglected. His granddaughter Elizabeth by Lady Audley was left only £50 per year in Sir John's will. (3) Lady Waterford considered this arrangement unfair and tried in various small ways to help her cousins; but Elizabeth suffered serious misfortune in later life and, despite help from Lady Waterford, was said to be living in poverty.

Susan, Lady Waterford, had lived the life of a respectable married women, so when she died in 1827, there was no scandal attached to her name - what a contrast to that of her mother, the wild Sarah, Countess Tyrconnel. Susan left the Ford estate to her son, Henry, then aged sixteen. He grew up to be known as 'Wild Henry', fond of hunting and racing. In 1842 Henry married Louisa Ann Stuart, daughter of Sir Charles de Rothsay. Henry and Louisa lived for a time at her family seat in Curraghmore in Ireland. Tragically Henry was killed in a riding accident in 1859. Louisa then returned to Ford and spent the rest of her life there improving the estate. She rebuilt Ford village but she is best remembered for painting the unique collection of Biblical scenes in Ford village school. The school, in use until 1957, is now known as Lady Waterford Hall. The outside of the building bears the coat of arms of the Beresford Family of whom the Marquis of Waterford is the head, and the Delaval motto Dieu me conduise. The Beresfords sold Ford Castle and its estates to the Joicey Family in 1907.

Apart from the legitimate family there were several illegitimate children to consider. Sir John also had at least one illegitimate grand child, Harry Jadis, of whom he was quite fond. He paid him an annual allowance of £100 and in his will left him an extra £300 a year. Harry became a close friend of Lord Strathmore and the last reference I have to him is at John Strathmore's wedding in 1820. (4) Sir John had also taken some responsibility for brother Francis's children, especially Frank. In his youth, Frank, like his father, was always in debt but as he matured he became more responsible. He joined the army and began a long career slowly rising through the ranks. In 1776, during the American rebellion, Francis was with his regiment in America. Sir John used his influence by writing to: 'His Excellency the Honourable General Sir William Howe, York Island, America…I owe your excellency for having given Mr Francis Delaval a commission and with very additional marks of your favour by appointing him to the first vacancy that happened after his arrival in America and in a regiment commanded by yourself.' (5) Sir John went on to congratulate General Howe on his success in America and he expressed his hope that the American Colonies would soon be back in the British Empire. Later Francis became a Captain in the corps of unattached officers. He became a Brevet Lt. Colonel in 1798, a full Colonel in 1808, a Major General in 1811 and a Lt. General in 1821. He married Mary Elizabeth, a widow with a small daughter, who had been married to a relative of Lord Tyrconnel. (6) Frank spent the last years of his life in the West Indies. His death, in 1826, on the Isle of Martinique was reported in The Gentleman's Magazine of that year. (7) Quite what he was doing there is not clear as Martinique was a French Protectorate at that time.

As the last members of the Delaval family faded away Seaton Delaval Hall, the birth place of this remarkable family, staged its most memorable performance. In the dim light of late afternoon on the 3rd January 1822, the Hall caught fire. The flames spread rapidly throughout the main block. The fire was visible for miles around and ships at sea noted the huge glow in the sky. A description of the fire was published in The Newcastle Chronicle on 5th January 1822: 'Every endeavour to preserve the body of the building was unavailing nothing but the bare walls being left standing. The fire is generally supposed to have originated in a chimney which had been rendered foul by birds having built their nests in it, and that hence the fire was communicated to a rafter fixed to the chimney.

The roof was speedily in flames and the fire burnt with such fury as to bid defiance to all human efforts. The glass in the windows, by the intense heat, was reduced to a liquid state and the lead in the roof poured down like water. The fire commenced its ravages about 4 o'clock in the afternoon…and it was not before 9 o'clock that the devouring elements could be checked.' (8) Hundreds of people rushed to the Hall to try to stop the flames and rescue what they could. Remarkably they saved the two wings but the fourteen rooms in the centre block and the southern extension to the East Wing were destroyed. (9) (The route of the fire can be traced by examining the sandstone walls. The heat of the fire changed the stone to a reddish colour and by following this trail the fire can be tracked.) (10) The servants and workmen brought out many movable objects including portraits, furniture and Sir John's boxes of papers. The papers found their way to an out-house at Hartley colliery and many years later they were again rescued from destruction, this time through neglect, by John Robinson as described in The Delaval Papers. When the fire was extinguished, the rescued items were taken into the two remaining wings but some smaller objects found their way into the houses of their rescuers. Over the years many of the objects have been returned including a painting which had been hidden under a bed for 80 years.

The centre block of the hall was roofless, the floors collapsed and the wonderful painted ceilings were gone. As the property was now owned by the Astley family of Melton Constable who did not use the hall very much, they would not pay to restore it. For much of the nineteenth century the house was neglected. Then in 1860 Sir Jacob Henry Astley instructed the Newcastle architect John Dobson to stop further deterioration and re-roof the fire damaged block.

The extensive red brickwork in the saloon dates from this period. However, it was not until about 1960 that the damaged roof was properly repaired. It is interesting to note that Dobson had drawn up plans to extend the hall around 1814 to 1817 but these extensions were never carried out. It was Sir Jacob who also revived the ancient family title of Hastings. Other branches of the family were claiming the title but in 1841 the House of Lords Privileges Committee reported in favour of Sir Jacob. So in May 1841, Queen Victoria called the Barony out of abeyance and Sir Jacob became the 16th Baron Hastings.

With the expansion of the railways, Seaton Delaval Hall and particularly the gardens became a tourist attraction. The Blyth and Tyne Railway advertised in 1851 that: 'A train will leave Percy Main for Seaton Delaval Gardens on Wednesday, Aug 20th at 12.30 p.m . Return to Percy Main 6.15 p.m. Fares First Class 1 shilling, Second class 9 pence. (11)

The Astleys spent very little on the Hall however they did use it. They occupied it from the end of the 19th century to the outbreak of the First World War. The Hall was used by the military in both World Wars and left in a very poor state. It was the late Lord Hastings who began the job of restoring the Hall.

In 1715 the Delavals were an unknown northern family on the edge of extinction. Sir John Delaval was virtually bankrupt and the house at Seaton was falling down. But within two generations they had built Seaton Delaval Hall, turned the small harbour at Seaton Sluice into a busy port and built an industrial complex exporting large quantities of glass bottles and coal. They modernised their estates. Several of them were elected to Parliament and John became a baron. Edward was a respected intellectual and friend of poets. Their love of the theatre brought the family much notoriety and the scandalous behaviour of some Delavals was noted in the newspapers of the time. They became friends and intimates of royalty. And then suddenly, they were gone! The estates were no longer owned by The Delavals. After 700 years their name had died out. That they survived as long as they did was perhaps due to the fact that they were fortunate in not getting too involved in national politics and simply good luck; but in 1814 their luck finally ran out. Laurence Whistler wrote: 'In this extraordinary house on a windy hill with an unkind sea at its foot there came to live an equally extraordinary family. They were the "gay Delavals", the most charming, mischievous, spendthrift people in the North of England, utterly without morals, loved by the people of the countryside and damned from birth.' (13)

Notes on chapter fourteen

1.   *For more information about other branches of the Delaval Family see Northumberland Families by Percy Hedley. In 1686 a Robert Delaval of Durham, was elected mayor of Durham. In 1689 he was removed by the Bishop of Durham on the grounds that he had become an embarrassment and had misapplied city revenues. The Surtees Society Vol CXI, 1905, p48.*

1A.   *The Proceedings of the Society of Antiquaries, Series 3, vol vi, 1913, p160*

2.   *Miscellany of Newcastle, Northumberland and the Borders by T. H. Rowland, 1986, p81*

3.   *Will of Lord Delaval. Berwick. R.O 2802/12. The copperas works closed about 1828, the brewery a few months later in 1829*

4.   *The Unhappy Countess, p167*

5.   *C.R.O. 2DE / 42/5*

6,   *North Country Lore and Legend, p283. The Gay Delavals, p186*

7.   *The Gentleman's Magazine, 1826, p647*

8.   *The Newcastle Chronicle 5th January, 1822*

9.   *East wing extension built 1770-72. Cost £3175 15s 4d. C.R.O. 2DE /4/4/56*

10.   *Archaeological Fire Investigation by Paul Murley. Paul is a fire safety officer with the Tyne Wear Brigade and has produced a technical report on the 1822 fire*

11.   *Miscellany of Newcastle, p82*

12.   *The Church of Our Lady was given to the Church of England in 1891 by Lord Hastings, and became the parish church, in the newly formed Parish of Delaval*

13.   *Sir John Vanbrugh, Architect and Dramatist 1938, p272s*

CHAPTER FIFTEEN
LORD HASTINGS

The late Lord Hastings, Edward Delaval Henry Astley, was born in 1912 in the family home in Melton Constable. A large house set in several thousand acres of farm land in Norfolk. The baronry goes back to the 1290s when Sir John Hastings was summoned to Parliament as Lord Hastings. The title became dormant in 1389 and eventually fell into abeyance. During the nineteenth century, several branches of the family tried to claim the title but after careful deliberation, the House of Lords Privileges Committee ruled in favour of Sir Jacob Astley. So, in 1841 the title was called out of abeyance and Sir Jacob became the 16th Baron Hastings. Edward became the 22nd Baron Hastings upon the death of his father in 1956.

Young Edward was educated at Eton. His domineering father did not believe he was capable of going to university so he travelled in Europe to improve his language skills. When he returned to London he tried City working for the Gold Coast Selection Trust and he also found time to join the supplementary reserve of the Coldstream Guards. He then went to America to America where he travelled 22,000 miles in fourteen months in a Ford V8 at a cost of 3 cents a mile. While he was in America the Second World War was declared but it wasn't until 1940 that he was able to get a passage home, where he re-joined his regiment.

After a year with the Guards, Edward was transferred to the Intelligence Corps which sent him to North Africa and then to Italy. In Milan he took over the local radio station and speaking fluent Italian, he was able to announce that the war had ended. At Trieste he ran both the theatre and local radio services. He ended the war with the rank of Major.

After the war he returned to the City and joined The London and Eastern Trade Bank. When this got into difficulties he went to Southern Rhodesia where he bought a 5,000 acre farm near Salisbury. Here he grew tobacco, peanuts and also some maize to feed the hundreds of workers and their families. It was while he was in Salisbury that he met former model Catherine Hinton, known as Nicki. Edward and Nicki married in 1954 and went on to have three children. Nicki also had two other children from her previous first marriage.

In 1956 his father died and Edward returned to Britain to take up his seat in the House of Lords. After four years he was appointed a government Whip and made Parliamentary Secretary to Sir Keith Joseph, then the Housing Minister. As a government Minister under MacMillan, he steered the Clean Air and

Water Resources Act through the upper house. The way he did this earned him the reputation as a safe pair of hands. He was also noted for his views on the situation in Rhodesia and was a stern critic of the Wilson government's handling of it. Lord Hastings served under several Tory governments and continued to attend the House of Lords until excluded by the Blair reforms of 1999.

Along with the title of 22nd Lord Hastings, Edward inherited Seaton Delaval Hall and about 6,000 acres of land. He also inherited the Norfolk estate but his father had sold the house at Melton Constable to pay off debts. However he still owned over 12,000 acres of land as well as property in Rhodesia. Delaval Hall was in a poor state of repair when he inherited it. The building had suffered years of neglect and during the last war it had housed German prisoners of war. Many windows had no glass in them and the centre block was too dangerous to visit. Edward set to work to repair and re-roof the house, while Lady Hastings attended to the gardens which were re-shaped and expanded. The parterre was laid out to the design of Mr J Russell of Sunningdale Nurseries in 1950 and the stone balustrade and twin steps were built by the Estate mason, Mr J Gardner. The dense shrubbery was cleared, opening up the view to the old church, lawns were laid and flowering shrubs such as rhododendrons and azaleas planted. It took four years and the help of a grant from the Historic Building Council before the Hall was made safe for the public to visit.

Lord and Lady Hastings furnished a flat in the west wing and they lived here for part of the year. Their first child, Harriet, was born in 1958 and their second child, Delaval, was born in Newcastle in 1960. In 1968 they had a third child, Justin, who has Downs Syndrome. This led to Lord Hastings becoming involved with the Camphill Village Trust, an organisation for people with learning difficulties. Eventually he gave them Thornage Hall in Norfolk and approximately 50 acres of land. Justin lives in the village and will be looked after by the Trust for the rest of his life.

In his long life, Lord Hastings helped many charitable organisations. He was President of the British Epilepsy Association (1965-1993) and Honorary President (1993-2007) of the Epilepsy Research Foundation and the Joint Epilepsy Council. His wartime experiences left him with a love of all things Italian. For more than forty years he was a Governor and Vice Chairman of the British Institute of Florence as well as being President of the British-Italian Society.

After Venice flooded he launched the Italian Peoples Food Appeal and was appointed a Grand Officer of the Italian Order of Merit for his efforts. He developed a passion for ballet and dance after visiting Covent Garden during the 1930s. He became friends with the leading ballerinas such as Margot Fonteyn and Beryl Grey. He became a Governor of the Royal Ballet and for more than twenty years he was Chairman of the Dance Teachers Benevolent Fund. Lord Hastings also supported local organisations and charities. He allowed the scouts and guides to camp on his grounds without charge. He was very fond of the Church of Our Lady and was Patron of the Parish of Delaval and a founder member of The Friends of Our Lady. He made generous donations to the Church. On the 900th anniversary of the church in 2002, he erected a large marquee in the grounds of the Hall and after the memorial service he entertained all the parishioners to a buffet lunch. No doubt there were other charitable gifts given of which I know nothing.

Lord and Lady Hastings spent a lot of time and money in restoring the Hall and gardens at Seaton. They sold their African properties in 1982 and spent less time in Norfolk. In the 1970s Medieval Banquets served in the old kitchen became very popular for a time. By 1990 the Medieval Banquets had finished, the Hall was re-decorated and then Lord and Lady Hastings made Seaton Delaval their permanent home. Lord Hastings opened the Hall to the public and it soon became a popular venue on the tourist route. At this point I would like to refer back to the old guide book written by Lord Hastings in which he acknowledged the "deep debt I owe to Mr Fred Hetherington, sub-agent of the Delaval Estates since 1946, whose initiative, careful supervision and practical assistance throughout the entire period.... which has seen the derelict home of the Delavals arise again almost like the phoenix from the ashes, have been of great comfort to me. Among other things Fred designed the new entrance gates and flanking walls which lead off the main road." Fred died in 1999 after being Lord Hastings' trusted agent for over 50 years.

In the latter years both Lord and Lady Hastings suffered from poor health, Lady Hastings suffered a stroke and was confined to a wheelchair for the last two or three years of her life. Lord Hastings devoted himself to her welfare but sadly he died suddenly in April 2007. Lady Hastings died the following December. They are both buried in the small graveyard in the garden next to the Church of Our Lady.

They left between them five children and as we have noted, Justin is in care. Their daughter Harriet has property in South Africa. She spends part of her year over there and part of the year in this country. The Astley property and titles passed to their eldest son, Delaval Astley. He has his own farming business in Norfolk. For the sake of the public's enjoyment and to keep the house and contents together in recognition of his father's lifelong commitment to the Hall, Delaval, Lord Hastings, commenced negotiations with the National Trust almost immediately after his father's death. After two years agreement was reached for the transfer of the Hall and some land. The Hall and contents were offered in lieu of tax and about 400 acres of land was bought by the National Trust. Contracts were signed in December 2009. The Trust opened the Hall to the public in May 2010.

With the death of Lord Hastings in 2007 another chapter closed in the life of Delaval Hall. For over 900 years the site has been under the control of either the Delavals or the Astley families. Now its fate lies with the National Trust. They have shown their commitment to the building by investing a great deal of money to re-roof, rewire and point the building. I hope they succeed in restoring the building and bringing it back to life.

Notes on chapter fifteen

Much of the information on the Astley family comes from unpublished documents. Some information on Lord Hastings comes from the daily Telegraph of May 5, 2007, and the Eastern Daily Press of May 10, 2007.

The late Lord and Lady Hastings in the rose garden at Seaton Delaval Hall (1998).

APPENDIX
Ghosts, Myth and Folklore

In a family with such a long history, stories are told which cannot be verified or sources traced. Some of these stories are recorded here. The only ghost in the Delaval story is the 'White Lady' whose apparition appears at an upper window on the North Front of the Hall. In certain lighting conditions, a white clad figure stands at the window looking down the drive, awaiting the return of a handsome young Delaval, who many years ago rode away from the Hall never to return. She may well have been a servant girl who fell in love and died of a broken heart when the marriage was forbidden.

For many years there stood an old stone by the track side a few hundred yards from Tynemouth Priory. The stone, known as the 'Monks Stone', was the pedestal of an ancient cross and the weathered remains still showed signs of elaborate carving. The stone was erected as a memorial to a monk at the spot where he was beaten to death by a Delaval. The story goes that the monk had visited the Delaval residence earlier in the day only to find his Lordship was out hunting. The cook had been given instruction to prepare a pig for dinner that evening. Now the monk was very fond of pork and while the cook was busy he stole the pig's head and made off back to Tynemouth. When his Lordship returned and was told of the theft, he became very angry as the head was his favourite part of a pig and in a rage he set off after the thieving monk. He caught up with him near the Priory and after beating him with his staff he retrieved the pig's head and returned home. Back at the Priory his brother monks alarmed by his absence went out to look for him and soon found him, more dead than alive. They took him back to the Priory where a few days later he died. Delaval was forced to pay compensation and the monks erected the stone cross on the site, inscribed on the stone were the words

O horrid dede

To kill a man for a pigg's hede (1)

There is another story about a standing stone which reputedly marks the spot where a Delaval caught a witch and is supposed to have carried her off and had her burnt at the stake! Holywell Dene, the deep and narrow valley, surrounding the Delaval estates has various tales of fairies and bogles. The streams and fields each had their own spirits. (2)

Stories of giants have been told since the Dark Ages but the Delavals had there own giant in Willie Carr, a blacksmith from Blyth. Willie was a real person but the stories about him are the stuff of legend. He was said to be able to lift the

Hartley Blue Stone, a large prehistoric stone monolith and leap a five-barred gate with the stone under his arm. On one occasion five seamen were told to take an anchor to the giant blacksmith for repair but they were unable to move it. Willie on hearing this went and swung the anchor on his shoulders and carried it back to the blacksmith's shop by himself, with the seamen following. Willie was said to be over 6 feet tall and to weigh over twenty four stone. Sir John had his portrait painted, so real he may have been although the stories told about him are the stuff of legend. (3)

The remains of Starlight Castle are still visible in Holywell Dene. The castle was supposed to have been built in twenty four hours, by starlight, as a result of a bet between Samuel Foote and Sir Francis Delaval. It was said that Foote bet Francis that he couldn't build a house in one day. Francis boasted he could build a castle in one day. So the bet was on and after careful preparation a team of builders using prepared stone, literally built this castle in a day and Francis won the bet. In the nineteenth century the castle was lived in but today it is just a crumbling ruin.

Note on Appendix One

1. *Bygone Northumberland p242*

2. *Hartley to Seaton Sluice, David Anderson, p14*

3. *Delaval Papers, p170*

NOTES ON SOURCES

The papers left by the Delavals were stored for many years in some buildings attached to Hartley Colliery. They lay neglected and were about to be destroyed when John Robinson rescued them. He published a selection of documents in the Delaval Papers (1880) which are now kept in the County Records Office at Woodhorn, Ashington. (C.R.O.)

The Earsdon Parish records list dates of birth, marriage and death in the family. These are also kept at the C.R.O.

Many 18th century letter writers and chroniclers mention the Delavals in their books, especially Horace Walpole in his diaries. Richard Edgeworth in his memoirs has some stories about Sir Francis and commentators on the life of the poet Thomas Gray mention Edward Delaval. The early history of the Delavals is recorded in A History of Northumberland Vol. IX. Mackenzie (1825) writes about Delaval Hall before the fire. The only book giving a full account of the eighteenth century family is The Gay Delavals by Francis Askham (1955). The library at The Literary and Philosophical Society of Newcastle contains many of the books mentioned in the Bibliography.

Books marked with a • mention the Delavals.

MANUSCRIPTS

The original documents left by the Delavals are sorted and listed in two large files. Those consulted are listed as at CRO.

BIBLIOGRAPHY

Allan Tom : Seaton Sluice and Old Hartley, a history in photographs 1992
- Anderson David : Sir John Vanbrugh, His Work in the North 1978
  Hartley to Seaton Sluice 1760 - 1960, Vol.1 1997
- Archaeologia Aeliana: Journals of the Proceedings of the Society of Antiquaries, Newcastle upon Tyne
- Astley Sir Edward: Seaton Delaval Hall, 1959
- Andrews William: Bygone Northumberland, 1899
- Arnold Ralph : The Unhappy Countess, 1957
- Askham Francis: The Gay Delavals 1955
- Bean William Wardell: The Parliamentary Representation of the Six Northern Counties of England, 1890
- Bickley A.C: The Gentleman's Magazine Library
- Birch James and Claire: Doddington Hall and Gardens
  Board of Agriculture -Answers to questions Re Ford Estate by J.Carr and J Oxley 1793 C.R.O
- Burgess Roger: Those Delavals! 1972
- Charlton Edward: Society in Northumberland in the last Century, 1874
- Coke Mary: Letters and Journals of Lady Mary Coke,1889-1896
- Cole R.E.G: History of the Manor of Doddington, Pigot 1897

- Cooke William: Memoirs of Samuel Foote, 1805
- Craster Herbert Henry: A History of Northumberland, Vol. VIII, 1907 and Vol. IX, 1909 Curnock Nehemiah: The Journals of John Wesley 1909 Danzinger Dany and John Gillingham: 1215 The Year of Magna Carta
- Delaval Sir John, Will 1806, Berwick Record Office
- Earnshaw Thomas: Hartley and Old Seaton Sluice 1961
- Earsdon Parish Records at C.R.O.
- Edgeworth Richard Memoirs of Richard L. Edgeworth begun by himself and finished by his daughter, 1820
- Foster R.A: The Industrial Development of Seaton Sluice 1948. A paper in Blyth Library.
- Fordyce T : Local Records, Remarkable Events 1876
- Garson William : Old Seaton Sluice and Delaval Hall. A pamphlet 1929
- Gatrell Vic: City of Laughter, Sex and Satire in 18th Century London 2006
- Graham Frank: The Old Halls Houses and Inns of Northumberland 1977
- Graham Frank: Newcastle A Short History and Guide, 1978
- Gray Thomas : Letters of Thomas Gray. Edited by D.C.Tovey 1900-1912
- The Diary of a Duchess, First Duchess of Northumberland. Edited by James Grieg, 1926
- Grenville George : The Grenville Papers. Edited by W. J. Smith 1852
- Hare Augustus: Two Noble Lives 1893
- Hedley Percy W: Northumberland Families, 1968
- Horsley P.M: Eighteenth Century Newcastle 1971
- Jackson G.W .Rev: The Church of Our Lady 1900 Revised 1997
- Joicey James: Ford at the time of the Waterfords 1822-1907, 1992
- Kapella W. The Norman Conquest of the North 1000-1135, 1997
- Ketton-Cremer R.W: Thomas Gray A Biography, 1955
- King Robert: North Shields Theatres, 1948
- Kirkman J.T: Memoirs of Charles Macklin, 1799 Lee Christopher : This Sceptred Isle 55BC-1901, 1997
- Linsley Stafford: Ports and Harbours of Northumberland, 2005
- Lomas Richard North-East England in the Middle Ages, 1992
- Lomas Richard County of Conflict Northumberland from Conquest to Civil war 1996
- Lord Chesterfield's Letters to his Godson. Edited By The Earl of Caernarvon 1889
- Mach L Thomas, Grey A Life, 2000
- Mackenzie E. An Historical, Topographical and Descriptive View of Northumberland, 1825 Miller Edwin: Eyewitness, The North East in Early Times, 1970
- Mitford John: The Correspondence of Thomas Gray and William Mason, 1855
- Moorhouse Sydney: Companion into Northumberland, 1953
- Murley Paul: Archaeological Fire Investigation. CD

- Namier Lewis: The Structure of Politics at the Accession of George III, 1929 Namier Lewis: The House of Commons 1754-1790, Vol.11 Parreaux Andre: Daily Life in England in the Reign of George III, 1966 Pevsner Nickolaus and Richmond Ian: The Buildings of England: Northumberland 1992
- Phillips Maberly: A History of Banks, Bankers and Banking in Northumberland, 1894
- Robinson John: The Delaval Papers, 1880
- Rowland T.H.: Miscellany of Newcastle, Northumberland and the Borders, 1983
- Stanhope Philip Dormer: Letters of Lord Chesterfield Ed. By Lord Mahon 1892
  Summers Judith: The Empress of Pleasure, 2003
- The Newcastle Chronicle 5th Jan. 1822
- Sedgwick Romney: The House of Commons 1715-1754 HMSO 1970
- The Meditations Of Lady Elizabeth Delaval, edited By D.G.Greene Published by the Surtees Society, 1978
- The Monthly Chronicle of North Country Lore And Legend, 1887
- The Publications of the Surtees Society, Vol. CXI, 1905
- Swinburne Henry: Courts of Europe at the close of the last century,1841
- Sykes John: Local Records or Historical Register of Remarkable Events, 1833
- Tillyard Stella: A Royal Affair 2006
- Tomlinson W.W : Denton Hall and its Associations, 1894
- Tomlinson W,W: Comprehensive Guide to the County of Northumberland, 1910
- Turberville A.S: The House of Lords in The Age of Reform 1784 –1837, 1958
- Toynbee P: The Correspondence of Thomas Gray, 1935
- Toynbee P: Letters of Horace Walpole, 1903-05
- Walpole's Correspondence; Edited by W. Lewis Vols.1-42
- Watts S. J: From Border to Middle Shire: Northumberland 1586-1625, 1975
- Welford Richard: Men of Mark Twixt Tyne and Tees, Vol 11, 1895
- Wells J.A : The Blyth and Tyne Railway, 1989
- Whistler Laurence: Sir John Vanbrugh, Architect and Dramatist, 1938
- Wills Margaret: Gibside and the Bowes Family, 1995
- Wilkinson Tate: Memoirs of his life, 1790
- Wraxall Nathaniel; Historical Memoirs of my Time, 1884

INDEX

135

INDEX CORRECTIONS